Spire Publishing

www.spirepublishing.com

Big Bloke, Small Boat: voyage of a madman?

by

William Garnier

Spire Publishing
www.spirepublishing.com

Spire Publishing, November 2008

First published in Canada and the UK 2008 by Spire Publishing.

A cataloguing record for this book is available from the Library and Archives Canada. Visit www.collectionscanada.ca/amicus/index-e.html

Designed in Salt Spring, Canada
by Spire Publishing Ltd.

Printed and bound in the USA or the UK
by Lightning Source Ltd.

ISBN: 978-1-926635-00-2

Spire Publishing

www.spirepublishing.com

"Live on the edge, it's where things happen" - Valentine Rawnsley

CONTENTS

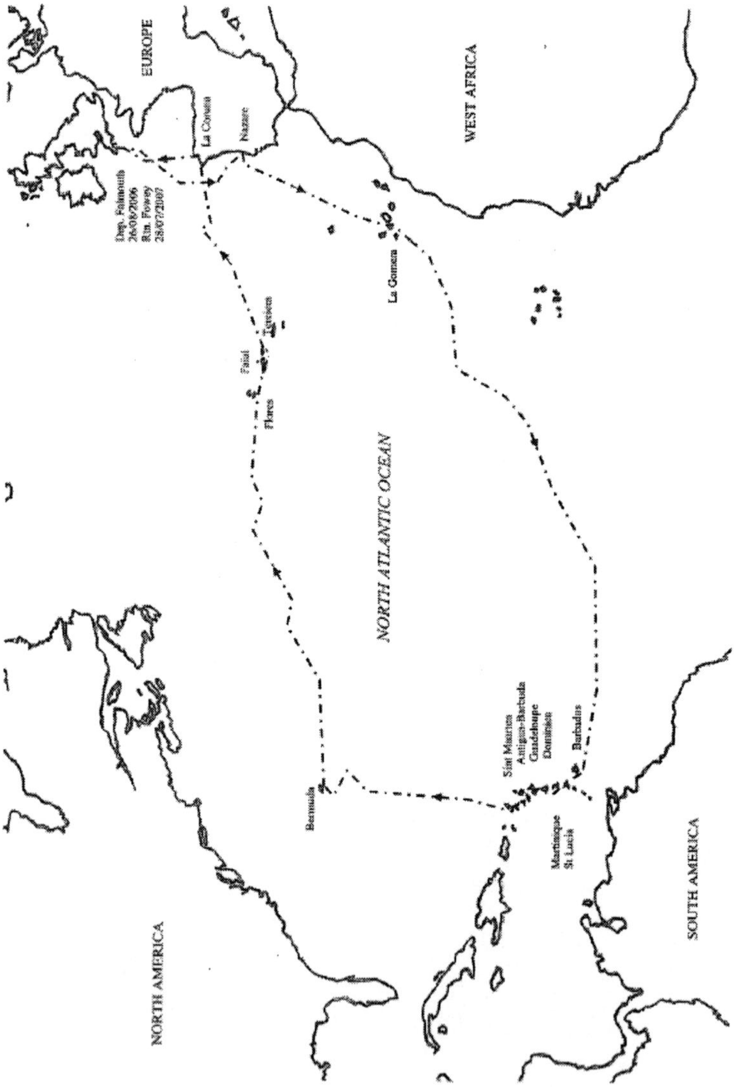
EUROPE
WEST AFRICA
La Coruna
Nazare
Dep. Falmouth
Rtn. Fowey
La Gomera
Faial
Terceira
Flores
NORTH ATLANTIC OCEAN
Bermuda
Sint Maarten
Antigua-Barbuda
Guadeloupe
Dominica
Barbados
Martinique
St Lucia
NORTH AMERICA
SOUTH AMERICA

Passage	**Date**	**Distance (Nautical miles)**	**Time at sea**	**Average speed (Knots)**
Falmouth, UK to Nazare, Portugal	26th Aug – 4th Sept 2006	786	9 days 2 hours	3.6
Nazare to San Sebastian, La Gomera	10th Jan. – 18th Jan 2007	801	7 days 12 hours	4.5
San Sebastian to Bridgetown, Barbados	29th Jan – 22nd Feb 2007	2800	24 days 4 hours	4.8
Bridgetown to Simpson Bay, Sint Maartin (via St Lucia, Martinique, Dominica, Guadeloupe, Antigua, Barbuda, St Kitts, Saba)	1st Mar. – 6th May 2007	470	4 days 12 hours (accumulated)	4.3
Simpson Bay to St Georges, Bermuda	15th May – 25th May 2007	1027	9 days 19 hours	4.4
St Georges to Porto das Lajes, Flores	5th June – 23rd June 2007	1861	18 days 11 hours	4.2
Porto das Lajes to Praia da Vitoria, Terciera (via Horta, Faial)	25th June – 5th July 2007	210	1 day 22 hours (accumulated)	4.5
Praia da Vitoria to La Coruna, Spain	9th July – 18th July 2007	949	9 days 4 hours	4.3
La Coruna to Fowey, UK	24th July – 29th July 2007	488	4 days 20 hours	4.2
Total		*9392*	*89 days 10 hours*	*4.3*

Introduction

It was never the plan to write a book about *Aluffe's* journey around the North Atlantic and the experiences we shared, but here it is, nonetheless. The appeal of technically stringing enough words and sentences together in a suitable order, no matter what the topic, so as to produce what constitutes a proper book has for long enough lurked in the back of my mind. Having something to say and being willing to say it, however, is another matter. The fact is, as a general rule, I am not drawn to the travel writing genre and nor am I confident enough about my own opinions to feel comfortable about displaying personal thoughts and feelings for all to read. Despite these reservations I returned to Cornwall in July 2007 appreciative of the fact that I had surely gathered together enough material to warrant an attempt. Flattered by the interest expressed by many people at my efforts and without a job or a particular desire to get one in the latter part of the year, it made sense for me to try formally ordering my views on the months that had past.

What follows is not a swashbuckling tale of daring-do where pirates abound and sea monsters run amok. What can I say? They didn't feature at all in the time I was away and I'm not sorry. Nor is it an in-depth technical breakdown that will satisfy the thirst of every widget and nuance orientated sailor seeking to cover all the bases and permutations of long distance cruising before one day embarking (or probably not) on their own adventure. Unfortunately for them my interest in that level of detail in anything has never been that strong. I have offered at least an insight into the lengths required to ensure *Aluffe's* seaworthiness and some of the practical problems others might also encounter. There are plenty of instructive and more informative boat manuals that can be used for complete tuition in the boat yard but, from the perspective of a relative newcomer to the cruising world, I trust elements within these pages will provide some helpful guidance.

7 months in a small boat is an intense experience, especially if a couple of ocean crossings are thrown into the mix of solitude, new horizons and an abundance of tinned squid. It was my reaction to this mix from which I learnt most and has made a lasting impression on me. Consequently I

have not shied away from being open about my responses to the highs and lows of the trip. I hope I have neither drudgingly laboured hardships where a stiff upper lip would have been more appropriate, nor attempted humour where it grates.

What I have tried to do is chart the preparations and comings and goings of my journey without embellishment, exaggeration or false modesty. To have noted panic where apprehension was more truthful, or a 10 metre wave instead of a realistic 5, would have served no purpose when most of all, my aim has been to put down an honest account of what it is really like to cross an ocean alone in a small sailboat.

Chapter 1
Biscay dream

Mention the Bay of Biscay to any whiskered elder wearing a bright yellow souwester and there will most likely be much sucking through the teeth, tut-tutting, and sagely shaking of the head. Perhaps there will also be a shuffling of the feet, an involuntary shiver in the shoulders, a weak moistening of the lips. Some will offer strangely terrestrial accounts of bridges being flattened by houses, whilst others might liken it to the road to Damascus. Indeed, mention the Bay to most seafarers of all ages, knowledgeable or otherwise, and it will conjure up a reaction that suggests something is not altogether right with the place.

Viewed on a chart and the area of sea nestling into the French Atlantic coastline, flanked by Spain to the south and Brittany to the north, appears blue and tranquil enough. It is not dissimilar, in fact, to many patches of sea around the globe which suggest peace and harmony. And yet, sitting at an end of the Atlantic fetch, across which the south-westerly prevailing winds and low pressure systems travel, the Bay can be seen in the same light as the buffers at the end of a rail track. It is the place where things stop because they have to. If that decisive point is reached before any significant effort to slow down has been undertaken, finding oneself in another place might be considered wise.

There is nowhere else for a large wave or fast moving train to go once the fetch or track has run out. Like a train hitting the buffers with a good deal of force, so the large waves generated and spurred on by the Atlantic storms create a mess when confronted by the sharply rising seabed and the confined space of the Bay of Biscay. With wave after wave tripping over the continental shelf before moving on to batter the French coastline order is lost and trouble can reign. It is in the Bay of Biscay that well founded boats and ships of all sizes are at risk from around 55 storms lasting a day or more each year. Bearing in mind that the average sailing boat will take 2 to 4 days to cross the area it is not surprising that sailors approach the Bay of Biscay with caution.

Announcing towards the end of 2005 my decision to attempt a circuit of the North Atlantic solo in my 24 foot sailing boat, *Aluffe*, it was obvious that not everyone thought it very sensible. *Aluffe* was definitely smaller than the average yacht crossing the oceans, and single-handed sailing has for a long while courted controversy. However, with boats less than 6 foot in length making it across the Atlantic, and a heavily sponsored offshore racing circuit for 22 foot boats in existence I didn't think my plan was so far-fetched. I soon became concerned, however, that the amount of advisory reading material offered to me by friends and family would dissuade the most ardent sailor, let alone me. I accept that, despite a background of family sailing holidays and club dinghy racing with a few championships and Channel crossings thrown in for good measure, I was perhaps not best qualified for the voyage. It was evident from the bulk of this literature, which could have occupied a shelf in a library entitled '*Disasters at Sea*', there were others in agreement. Stories of boat losses, drowned crews, rogue waves, capsizes, piracy and simple disappearances were thrust upon me in such numbers that I could not help but question some of the motives behind the initial generosity. It seemed that the library shelf would have been more appropriately named '*These terrible things and more, William, happen at sea! Don't go!*'

If the idea was to scare me off my plan, it didn't work. If the words of wisdom and experience were designed to focus my preparations with safety in mind then they were heeded, so much so, in fact, that I booked myself on to a sea survival course. It was on that course that an experienced skipper gave his first hand account of the time he watched, unable to help, as one of his crew drifted away from the safety of the liferaft after a storm in the Bay of Biscay had capsized their 40 foot yacht. Only the lifejacket of the unfortunate crewman was later recovered by the rescue helicopter. I was not complacent or lacking in my preparations but it was with these accounts of trouble at sea in mind that I too approached the Bay of Biscay with caution.

Mistrusting a lazy streak that speaks favourably of chocolate and television I am driven more by a love for the outdoors and the pleasure of feeling healthy. I have subsequently made some effort to remain active and to push my physical boundaries, chequering my 38 year history with the welcome challenges of long cycle rides and other endurance events. The difference between taking part in land based sports in the main and sailing in the middle of the ocean, however, is that you can't easily get off a boat on a whim. If one tires in a running race there is the option of stopping to end the discomfort. The options available to a sailor are less obvious or palatable. Having spent many years competing against others and racing the clock I was looking for the motivation of a new trial.

The appeal of an ocean crossing to me was the need to be resourceful in an arena that is not contrived. The difficult bits of a marathon course are known before the event starts, unlike a sea passage which could encounter any number of storms at any stage along the way. It could be argued that the risks and stakes are higher at sea. Whilst a marathon runner might have to overcome tiredness, blisters and a fear of failure, an offshore sailor, without the benefit of immediate assistance if there is gear failure or injury, can deal more closely with issues like death or survival. Such choices do not, thankfully, occur too often and it must be remembered that for ever the seas have been used by explorers, traders, and tourists. In amongst the worst storms and tempestuous seas countless journeys have been successfully completed, far outstripping the unfortunate number that has not. To find a near death experience was never the goal but I did want to discover how resourceful I could be in a more challenging and natural environment.

That opportunity first arose when I eventually crossed the Bay of Biscay for the first time in late August 2006. Whilst I might have reasonably hoped to pass through unscathed at that time of year it came as no surprise that my arrival coincided with that of a gale. Slipping my moorings at Falmouth 3 days beforehand I made rapid progress out of the Channel and the Western Approaches with a forceful blow from the north-west. Exciting sailing though it was I suffered from sea sickness on a grand scale. Unable to hold any solids or liquids down I was feeling the worse-for-wear. Given that I was also wet, cold and definitely out of my comfort zone some 160 miles from land I listened with interest to the forecast warning of the approaching gale. Perhaps it was because of my low energy levels but I took the news calmly enough. Despite being well aware of the Bay's particular reputation for causing damage and habit for taking lives I reminded myself that panicking was unlikely to help. *Aluffe* was comfortably afloat and behaving as might have been expected at that time. She was moving about a lot but there was no immediate or apparent danger of sinking. So it was more with curiosity than concern that preparations were made for a night of new experiences.

Just as there are, allegedly, many ways to skin a cat so there are countless approaches to tackling heavy weather at sea. Not having tried any method for the former I suppose factors such as the sharpness of a knife (if indeed a knife was to be involved), the toughness of skin, the desire of the chosen feline to be skinned and, subsequently, the ease of its catching would, amongst others, all have a bearing on a successful, or otherwise, outcome. Likewise, boat size, number of crew, size of waves, strength of wind, length of fetch, depth of water, and many more factors all have their role to play in engineering a plan to deal with the big stuff at sea.

The more common approaches would include running before the wind and waves with an appropriate spread of sail. Dragging a drogue or warps and fenders at the same time to slow the boat would be considered good practice if the occasion demanded. Letting out a sea anchor (effectively a large parachute) from the bow in order to hold the boat in position, whilst offering the sharpest point of the boat to part the waves, is another option. A third tactic would be to heave-to. This amounts to a controlled drift where the boat, with minimal sail set, is held in a position at almost 90 degrees to the wind. The latter 2 options allow the crew to shelter below and avoid the debilitating effects of breaking waves and high winds. The first option of sailing downwind normally requires the crew, me on this occasion, to drive, exposed to the elements.

Without food and drink for nearly 3 days tiredness was rapidly becoming a factor and to take either of the 2 'shelter' options was sensible. Knowing this, but having less faith in the heave-to tactic, the sea anchor was pulled from its locker and placed centre-stage in readiness for its turn in the limelight. Weakened by illness, however, doing any more proved too much. Having laid everything out in the cockpit I drifted vacantly into a state of mental pause where the extent of my cerebral and physical activity amounted to merely low level observation. I 'woke up' 30 minutes later without any progress having been made and all the kit required for a proper deployment still in a tangled pile at my feet. My first ever gale, in, horror of horrors, the Bay of Biscay, was due imminently and I was galvanizing myself less effectively than a perplexed ostrich.

Still sitting in the cockpit when the gale arrived a little while later and having got no further with my bad weather preparations there was no alternative but to sail through the night for as long as possible before wilting. An ostrich can stick its head in the ground and the world will pass it by until, eventually, something will bite it on the bum. At that time it will make a decision, possibly to run away very fast. My head-in-the-sand moment came not just with the waiting for the gale to arrive but also with how long I could remain at the helm. My bum was firmly nibbled when the gale arrived and comprehensively chewed at 0400 hours the next day, 10 hours after first hearing of the gale's approach. Sleep took hold and the decision was made for me. I hove-to and slept below. Waking up 2 hours later I lay for a moment on the cabin floor listening to the wind powering through the rigging and feeling the boat being lifted by the waves. I sat up and looked out of the window, blinked at the shock of my life, and then fairly flew into the cockpit. Grabbing the sea anchor tackle on my way out to the bow, I secured one end, and hastily threw it over board.

Some of the books I read before leaving had pictures in them. One in particular described more scientifically the nature of weather at sea. It explained the Beaufort Scale, the scale universally used around the world to indicate not only wind speed but the relative state of the sea, even indicating what sail plan sailboats should carry for each occasion. The Beaufort Scale runs from 0 to 12, where 0 is 'nothing happening' and 12 is 'there is no 13'. A gale is registered at 8 on this scale and, whilst dinghy sailing is not recommended, in the open sea with deep water below and little, if any, land around about a well founded yacht could consider this to be testing conditions. Something to get your teeth into with caution. This I now know but not at my first sighting through the cabin window of conditions which compared favourably with the pictures in the book describing the Beaufort Scale. Confronted for the first time with ominously grey, spray streaked impositions of water standing some 5 metres tall bearing down on *Aluffe* got my attention. Thoughts of being knocked down and capsized flashed through my mind as *Aluffe* was positioned with her port side exposed to the face of those monstrosities. Making the sensible decision to get the sea anchor out in an attempt to pull the bow into the waves was relatively simple. More importantly under the circumstances I readily found the energy to carry it out immediately.

As it was the sea anchor was fairly useless being too small and had a negligible effect on the boat's position. She remained largely beam on to my concern and continued to drift at a similar rate across the main shipping routes between the north-west points of France and Spain. I watched at first with some dismay and worry. I challenged my sleep and nutrition-deprived brain for an answer but soon realised that an answer was not necessary. Inadvertently I had discovered that *Aluffe* was more settled hove-to in these conditions than on the end of the 'anchor'. The waves were big but, being well spaced, I began to see that they posed no threat. They did not break at the top and there was minimal risk of *Aluffe* getting knocked on her side, rolled, or even swamped in those conditions. I sat back, appreciatively, admiring the surroundings. *Aluffe* slipped down into each trough, the wind dropping off slightly, before she rose smoothly up the long face of the following wave and back into the full breath of the wind. I had not eaten in days and was no drier than the night before but, looking about and seeing only grey skies and powerful seas surrounding my solitary little boat, I was compelled to smile: this was a surprisingly good moment. Any discomfort I felt mattered not a jot. Bobbing up and down all alone, miles from land and all the security and distractions it provided, was immensely satisfying.

For many years I have had a recurring image in my mind, that of being on a large yacht driving into the full force of a turbulent ocean sea. The bow ploughs into an oncoming wave, the boat shudders, and water is forced impressively to either side and over the boat while it rises and then falls down hard into the space below before repeating the process. There is no mistaking the awesome, unremitting power of the waves impacting on the solid but otherwise comparatively feeble boat. Sometimes my arms are outstretched in the face of the oncoming wind in a foolishly dramatic 'come and get me, I'm not hiding' kind of way.

What the imagery generated by my absent mind actually means is not obvious but there is never any doubt that the ocean certainly could get me if circumstances prevailed. This is backed up by historical records and the many anecdotes handed down by seafarers over time. There can be surely no doubt that the worst sea would trump the best boat. In that regard the mere notion of being at sea is a very serious proposition. Growing up in a time and place of central heating, comfy shoes and electric bread knives it is possible to fret about life being, physically at least, too cosy and easy. I take some comfort in knowing that parts of the world remain inhospitable and pose a challenge to those attempting to pass through. Such places demand respect and offer the opportunity to test one's mettle. It is in part for that reason that I was drawn to plan and carryout my Atlantic circuit.

Waiting for the gale to subside and allow me to continue on my way I had the chance to acknowledge how potent the sea could be. The energy in the water around me was nothing if not impressive. I was respectful of that insight granted to me of the Bay of Biscay's reputation. There was no disguising the fact that unprepared, as I almost was given my health, the proverbial could really hit the fan at sea. And yet, wearing my rank and soggy hair shirt, I noted that it hadn't. The gale had not been a storm or worse and if there was a wave out there with my name on it, then it had not passed by that day. No houses had borne down on me and there had been no call to seek the assistance of an omnipotent power.

I was in fact, in the manner of that most horrible of expressions, realising a dream. A force of nature, against which I could only do my best, was being confronted in scenes similar to those which I had imagined. Ultimately, my best could never be enough but by controlling all that I possibly could about the boat and within myself I stood a better chance of achieving my aim. It seemed I was doing enough so far.

It dawned on me properly then that my lonely jaunt across the seas would be far more of a mental test than one based on the physical alone. Pulling bits of string and driving the best course would be useful skills but rendered useless if I allowed myself to become exhausted or prepared the boat poorly in the face of bad weather. Learning the critical art of boat management and, more importantly, self management would be the keys to successfully completing the course. On this first test the weather had been lenient and some right answers had been stumbled upon. Top marks could not be claimed but I felt no less privileged to be so apparently isolated and coping in such a powerful environment. Some good, some bad. On balance I was feeling really quite positive and very definitely up for more.

Chapter 2
Day sailor or offshore cruiser?

It is a curious thing that *Aluffe*, an Achilles 24 built in 1975, was bought on the recommendation of my girlfriend, Jacqui, who knew marginally more than nothing about sailing at the time. It was she who ducked below into the cabin of a friend's Cornish Shrimper we were borrowing in 2002 and returned with a sandwich and a pack of crisps.

"Would you like some?" she asked with a smile.

Had it been any of a number of other times the offer would have been gratefully accepted. However, as we were approaching the gybe mark in a race out of St Mawes I refused, harbouring dark thoughts at her disconcerting lack of awareness. Certainly, it was a beautiful Cornish evening and the one-off race for us was of little consequence. Whilst others in the competitive fleet of 5 were concentrating wholly on winning precious points in the Thursday night Summer series and a free pint in the bar afterwards, my focus of attention should have been directed more towards cementing our new relationship.

But I had pedigree. I had reached the dizzy heights of a mid-fleet finish at the Fireball World Championships in 1997. Not long after in 1999 I shared the accolade of J24 National Team Champion. The fact that I was more keen than able on both occasions, relying on the skills of those around me to improve my standing in the racing scene, is of little importance. The fact was I held the position of Master and Commander aboard the good Shrimper '*Pisces*' on that day and was clearly the only one of the 2 of us on board who knew what was what about sailing. Therefore, when suggesting a few days later I might get back into sailing properly and buy myself a small sailboat to enjoy the

Cornish coastline and estuaries, it remains a mystery as to why I listened to Jacqui.

"You should get an Achilles 24," she stated helpfully, not hiding for one moment that her opinion had been formed on the basis of her only afternoon of sailing a few years before being on such a vessel. I had never come across these boats before but Jacqui had previously pointed out an Ajax 23, an attractive 3-person racing boat, gliding appealingly swiftly down the Carrick Road towards Falmouth.

"It's like one of those," she said, adding, "with a lid on."

It would have been both unfair and fruitless to press her for more detail as I could see the extent of her knowledge was exhausted. I was mildly humouring her when I picked up the local rag and checked for boats not long after. If I was also being slightly patronising this attitude began to evaporate with the appearance of an Achilles for sale in the classifieds. Not only was it for sale at a reasonable price but it was located a short 20 minutes away from our home.

I am not a great follower of things spiritual and find little empathy with those pushing the notion of fate. 'It was meant to be' seems a wholly unsatisfactory cornerstone to the reason for our being and subsequent actions. Sadly, I am of small brain and every time an attempt has been made to put some meaningful flesh on the otherwise meagre bones of life in the past, confusion has always been the net result. I live in hope that one day, probably my last, the answer will become a little clearer. Nevertheless, the sequence of events that led me to a secluded farmyard on the banks of the River Lyhner to find *Aluffe* did seem more than simply fortuitous.

Looking at her for the first time nestled into a corner of the farm pressed in amongst a fine crop of nettles and a range of farm detritus I might have been forgiven for extending my thanks to the prospective vendor and making haste to leave. Resting precariously on the rusting trailer assigned to her, her sleek lines bore the marks of a boat that had not been sailed for some time and was short of tender loving care. Her single mast and boom lay by her side in a muddled web of wire, while deep green mould coated the wooden strips running along her length. Antifoul was pealing in thick layers off her hull and rust unashamedly spread itself about the cast iron fin keel. Over time leaves had been allowed to settle into the nooks and crannies of the deck and fittings. There was evidence of metal fatigue and the windows could claim no more than a season of good service left to give. And yet, many of my first impressions were superficial on closer inspection. There was never any question that work would have to be done before her first season in new hands. Beyond that, however, the sleek little boat, with her low cabin and long cockpit, was largely intact and ready for another go after nearly 4 years of inactivity.

Most importantly, I quickly fell into the 'right' zone occupied by people like me where, having sought and found something that is a passably close approximation of our desire, we are beguiled by how 'right' everything feels. Any glaring deficiencies in the potential purchase are entirely ignored by promoting to the heights every insignificant positive without shame. Pursuing the cause seems 'right' despite not really being able to give any convincing argument in support. Before long we, the vendors dream, are paying the money and backing our decision by merely claiming it is the 'right' thing to do.

Only a few weeks separated the initial expression of interest in buying to actually handing over good money for *Aluffe*. Searching for her and finding her had been remarkably easy. It had been as smooth as smooth processes go. Even agreeing a price had been succinct.

"I'll offer you £2600," I said.

"The asking price is £3000," he said.

"Will you accept less?" I said.

"No," he said.

You can't argue with that; job done. I laughed at having so easily taken on the trappings of a would-be man of status. The process of doing so had been swift and emboldening. I was the owner of an 'ocean-going yacht' I had joked, blissfully unaware of how right I was and how very serious I would become.

I have never seen any original publicity material but I suspect in the mid-seventies the Achilles 24 was pushed upon the growing leisure sailing market at the family end. The design does have 4 berths, a galley, and a navigation station. There are even ensuite facilities for the vertically challenged in the forepeak. However, by today's standards the Achilles is fantastically small inside. Volume can surely not have been a term often used in the early days of modern yacht design, particularly in relation to living space. Headroom in the main cabin is 4 foot 6 inches and the boat is only a fraction wider than I am tall. Standing at 6 foot 6 inches I had to quickly come to terms with these obvious disadvantages when down below. As Jacqui had correctly pointed out the Achilles, even with its cabin, was similar to the Ajax 23 which was a graceful open boat designed for racing and day sailing. To those not familiar with the history of the Achilles, which included me at the time, *Aluffe* was, at 24 feet in length, not so much a yacht but a glorified dinghy.

I quickly came to realise that to suggest the Achilles was anything less than an accomplished and fast sailing vessel that punched well above her weight was an injustice and quite false. She is a well-balanced sloop design that looks evenly proportioned, strong, and seaworthy. In practice she is all of these things and to prove it has a few ocean crossings attributed to her design. It was not uncommon for complete strangers to stop alongside on the pontoons in order to gaze admiringly at her, often passing judgement. This is not so strange in that yachties invariably feel it is perfectly within their rights to comment at great length about everyone else's pride and joy. What struck me most was that their comments about *Aluffe* were never anything other than favourable. It is always pleasing to have confirmed the correctness of one's choice but I suspect with each comment, sub-consciously at least, I developed a growing belief in *Aluffe* and the possibility of real adventure.

In the early days, however, feeling pleased with my new acquisition and the thought of cruising the length of the Cornish coast, exploring the multitude of estuaries, coves, and ports, I was content to busy myself getting her ready for her first season in my care. When it came to the launching, a friend sailed his 38 foot yacht over to Fowey from Plymouth before joining me up-river for *Aluffe*'s first journey towards the sea. The plan was to stop in Fowey on the first night before taking her on the next day to the Helford Estuary where a mooring had been secured off the pretty village of Durgan. Rafting up alongside Nick's boat after a successful launch the harbourmaster, seeing activity, came over to collect the dues owed by Nick. As that transaction came to its natural conclusion the harbour master looked over towards *Aluffe* - my super yacht *Aluffe*.

Most people jump at the chance when offered something for free but on the suggestion to Nick that he would 'let the tender go for free' I allowed pride to take over some control of my emotions and actions. This was my first command for which good money had been paid and over which I had sweated honestly in my efforts to prepare her for a reintroduction to the Cornish scene. Just as the mega-rich in their vast gin palaces want the general riff-raff to acknowledge the fruits of their power and good fortune I too wanted the respect of the yachting industry, if only because I momentarily felt *Aluffe* might be offended. To refer to her as 'the tender' was to suggest we had not yet 'arrived'. True or otherwise I was going to pay my way and be counted.

Cometh the hour, however, to claim my place at the high table of respectability I probably realised that there was little value in it and *Aluffe* and I would be better off making our mark in other, as yet undefined, ways. It is true that whilst my hand searched frantically for my wallet in an effort to see *Aluffe* officially recognised and to restore my dignity I didn't actually pull it out very quickly. My faux indignation was eventually satisfied with some liberal huffing and puffing along with some rather dubious hand activity in my pockets. I think I made my point, anyhow.

There was never any real plan behind the use of *Aluffe*. It seemed sensible to get aboard her as often as possible with a view to familiarising ourselves with the few systems and her sailing qualities. Most weekends Jacqui and I would fill the car with our phenomenally large overnight bags, food, tender, and other paraphernalia commonly associated with the weekend sailor. In the following years this would also include an ever lengthening dog. Each trip down involved a laborious process of pumping up the dinghy, dragging it down the beach, filling it with some of our gear, paddling to the mooring, offloading, returning to pick up the remaining gear and transferring it to *Aluffe*. The dinghy was then deflated and stowed until the next occasion of disembarkation and inflation. After all that messing about Jacqui would often make a cup of tea as a final delaying tactic, but we would eventually set off to enjoy the drama and tranquility offered by the superb Cornish and Devon coastlines.

Cornwall can get overcrowded and spoilt in the summer months with the arrival of literally millions of tourists. The county swells to gargantuan proportions. Inconvenient and even unpleasant though this can be to those who see the county in all its guises over the full course of a year it is perfectly understandable. From the harsh landscape of the historically rich clay mines, through the steep-sided valleys, and into the oak woodlands lining the picturesque rivers and estuaries Cornwall has conjured up an appeal that is virtually unrivalled anywhere in the United Kingdom. For sailors there are secure shelters from bad weather and a multitude of inlets, coves, harbours and other sheltered anchorages suitable for the explorer and day sailor alike. Each stopping point is never too far from a landing and a pub. Having been stuck mainly onshore before taking possession of *Aluffe* it did not take long to realise the benefits of a boat in amongst such jewels. We could never have hoped to discover all the best places open to us, even though we tried, but somehow Jacqui and I still managed to find ourselves instead sailing to the Channel Islands in that first season.

There was good reason enough for the trip in the form of a friend who was due to finish a leg of The Clipper Round the World Race in St Hellier, Jersey. The desire to welcome him across the line after all his efforts was strong enough but having, all of a sudden, a yacht with which to make the journey as well, signed and sealed it for me.

It was clear from our shorter excursions that summer we still had work to do on *Aluffe* in order to get her up to scratch. The engine and electrics were temperamental, and the halyards had a remarkable capacity to stretch under load. The sails had certainly done time at sea and we were very short of contemporary navigational aids beyond a chart and hand bearing compass. But, as I keenly pointed out, she had no problem floating, we knew where we wanted to go, and how to get there. However, size of boat, big waves and even bigger boats, particularly those more commonly found in the shipping lanes, became issues that had to be overcome before Jacqui, my sole crewmate, was convinced. In truth, I cannot recall how these were in the end beyond some visible tinkering with the engine and the purchasing of a GPS and a fog horn. I threw into the ring as evidence of my competence my 2 previous experiences of crossing the Channel but still relied heavily on something which lay in the magic found in a small good-looking boat.

Even if she wasn't in the best of condition at that time, and skippering was new to me, *Aluffe* gave the impression that she could, and we should, cross the 90 miles to Jersey. It is a trust and relative confidence thing that makes for a persuasive case. To accept the verdict is, and was, liberating and energising. I became aware of the appeal in stretching beyond my experience, having the confidence to take Jacqui with me, and feeling no doubt. Some of this must have come from the potential that radiated from the good design that *Aluffe* represented. I think I saw then, towards the end of the summer of 2003, that *Aluffe* had so much more to offer as an 'ocean going yacht' than as a glorified dinghy. Taking umbrage at the Fowey harbourmaster's good natured jibe did not seem so much of an overreaction after all.

Depending on who one talk's to, the trip to Jersey from Salcombe was a complete disaster bar for the fact we didn't sink. Instead of the 22 hours promised it took 36, largely due to the incompetence of the skipper who had not filled up with enough diesel to be used in the event of a dying wind, which it did when the fog came in. The situation was not improved by said skipper's attempts to cheer the crew up with the obvious game of Scrabble, when, sitting in the shipping lanes, he should have been concentrating on other things. It was no less comforting when he jumped overboard to check the propeller was clear of weed. Finding him hallucinating towards the end of his first 30 hours on the helm hardly helped the situation either. Under the circumstances, dolphins playing on the bow were never going to be distraction enough as the Condor ferry thundered past 200 metres off the stern. It should, therefore, have been no surprise when tears flowed unchecked once the large, clean, and, critically, land-based hotel room was finally reached.

There remains some debate about whether the coastguard or the aforementioned incompetent skipper was at fault for a breakdown in communication with friends ashore but if one asked me I would say the trip was brilliant. Of course things didn't go quite to plan. Mistakes were made, and I wouldn't do it like that again. A list as long as my arm could be drawn up by the aficionados of all the things that would be classed as dubious to appalling seamanship and I wouldn't be able to deny many of them. If someone told me they were going to repeat our trip across the Channel in all its naivety I would question the wisdom of their decision. But I wouldn't think any less of them for trying if it meant they learnt as much as we did in achieving something that proved to be such an exhilarating stepping stone. For every mistake made a lesson was learnt.

I remind myself of the 3 main reasons why I thought we could go in the first place – *Aluffe* floated, we knew where to go, and how. Where 2 out of 3 are considered not bad, we did very well to get 2.5. Most importantly we got to St Hellier and in so doing proved that there is great mileage to be made when a healthy dose of enthusiasm is mixed with a trust in the basics. In the aftermath of the trip there was some gentle criticism directed towards me, most of which was accepted gracefully because I knew it to be right. But it was important for me never to forget that had I known everything I learnt during the trip before leaving I probably never would have. The benefits of learning on the hoof were obvious and justified the risk.

Jersey was a lovely island which we did not have time to explore what with the triumphant arrival of the reason for our being there and then our need to get home. Given her experiences getting to Jersey Jacqui pumped herself up admirably and stuck it out for the return leg. In stark contrast to the admittedly slow passage out, *Aluffe* sprouted wings and Salcombe was reached 19 hours later. Once again the experience was thrilling as *Aluffe* launched herself at the sea as if without a care in the world. Not since my days' dinghy racing had I had so much fun on the water as we surfed down waves with the moon lighting our way. The shipping lanes were negotiated without mishap although we nearly came a cropper on a very large and slow moving Basking shark. If contact had been made it is far from certain that the shark would have come off worst.

Once again, however, exhaustion was in the ascendancy by the end and I made a mental note to get a grip on the watch systems. So tired were we when we scrambled onto the visitors' pontoon that we only realised that neither of us had a mooring line in our hand as the boat began to drift away on the tide. Relief to be ashore is one thing but I made another mental note to maintain a better grip on the boat in the future. For sure, I didn't want to let her go.

There followed 2 seasons of local exploration during which time much was learnt about a superlative cruising ground but more again about *Aluffe* and what it was that she could offer. Her simplicity was invaluable in that not only was there little to maintain but little with which to fiddle before setting off to one anchorage or another. Being of relatively shallow draught at 4.5 feet we could tuck her in close to the shore away from the bigger boats. Her diminutive size and simplicity were, however, something of a double edged sword. Whilst they allowed us to manoeuvre her into tight mooring spots they did not always lend themselves to a comfortable night having arrived. Overall she is thin and light which meant that she could be described as tippy. Sit either side of the centre line and she would noticeably lean in response. Not so bad but it also meant that a swell or passing boat would cause *Aluffe* to wobble about. That characteristic coupled to an interior with a volume akin to that of a squashed 4-man tent and patience would occasionally be at a premium. It meant that trips any longer than a weekend had to be carefully planned. The weekend trips themselves were never quite as relaxing as they might have been had *Aluffe* been longer and wider with enough room for pillows on larger bunks. But that was not *Aluffe* and, besides, it was her qualities under sail that were most impressive.

As well as on the Channel crossing *Aluffe* proved herself time and again to be very assured and efficient underway. There was no disguising her actual stature but her behaviour suggested she was so much more. What with the appreciative looks and comments of fellow sailors and her pace to all points of the compass I must have, in those first few seasons, gradually absorbed a notion that *Aluffe* could really go places. Moreover, she could really take me places.

'She crossed the Channel; imagine if we had stayed there', I thought. 'We could potter along the French coast to Spain and Portugal. Now we are heading somewhere', I thought, 'and it could all be done by day sailing. The Mediterranean could be the next stop or Africa. What about the Caribbean? These boats have crossed oceans before, why not *Aluffe*? Why not me?'

I thought.

The winter months invariably included a few spent fixing and upgrading the boat. As well as learning the skills of boat maintenance and the greater value of knowing someone with an enormous tool box and heart to match, I began to appreciate how boats are invariably extensions of their owners and can represent the limits of their ambition. For a boat can be so much more than a simple mode of transport on water. In a world where the majority of us live sedentary lives a boat can take us beyond horizons and to distant places of our choosing. Not only do they move but they can take our kit with us, and in some style. Campervans do the same but they have to follow set routes whereas the freedom of movement possible in a boat is not replicable.

Boats are as varied as garden sheds in their uses and looks. Whilst one man cherishes his sleek racing machine, polishing it as only a naval officer can polish his shoes, another will claim the kettle to be the most valuable thing on board. Some will demonstrate their wealth by purchasing the largest and shiniest yacht available, and others will use theirs to showcase boat skills and knowledge learned over a lifetime of sailing. Whatever the motivation that drives people to own boats each reason is disarmingly honest.

I was certainly glad of all the help offered to me. My main tactic for tackling boat maintenance generally involved a considerable amount of looking and prodding before approaching the chosen problem with a drill, hammer, and a tube of sticky marine filler. It was not uncommon for oaths and other unmentionables to be thrown far and wide as I relished in the care of my charge on rainy weekends. Despite those instances, I never tired. I claimed as much on enough occasions and only just restrained myself from putting *Aluffe* on the market more than once. Each time, however, I could not ignore that I had enjoyed learning something new, something that not only improved my knowledge but also the capacity of *Aluffe* to become an even more accommodating sailboat. With each stripped thread and grazed knuckle, a difficulty was overcome and a problem solved. There was always progress which in turn was heartening. It maintained motivation and kept me going, even when the destination was not accurately known.

Moving *Aluffe* to a mooring in Falmouth for the summer meant that she was closer to our home further east. This enabled us to get aboard with a fraction less fuss and excursions up and down the coast continued.

The dog persisted in growing and we narrowly avoided being obliterated by the Fowey Regatta fireworks one evening, but small bays and quiet harbours still played host to *Aluffe* and her entourage.

Over time, however, I noticed a hassle factor creeping into our trips. Perhaps we were beginning to repeat ourselves too often and becoming too familiar with our regular haunts. Maybe the trips became normal and no longer stretched our imagination. Certainly I became less tolerant of all the fuss associated with the dinghy. The spice that previously surrounded our weekends was less tangible, especially so as *Aluffe* went about the business of being a sailing boat with such assuredness. We did not appear to be pushing her boundaries. My understanding that she was a boat capable of far more than mere coastal hopping became ever more acute as each extra mile passed under her keel.

I frequently sailed her overnight and often on my own. Every time I watched the Cornish coast slipping by I questioned why it could not be the shores of a foreign land. All the usual suspects were raised – relationship, work, money, boat, time, etc – and while each held a varying degree of water, none ever managed to swamp a burgeoning excitement within me. I suppose it was only a matter of time before I stopped looking for answers as to why not and focused more on finding reasons why.

For a long time, a matter of years, in fact, I had harboured an interest in 'doing something different'. Whilst I have demonstrated myself to be extremely good at conforming to the general rules of a modern western society on the whole, I have never been entirely comfortable with it either. As a result there has been a tendency to rub along with those things nurtured before what I would consider a moment of nature kicks in. Consequently my life has an element of the boom and bust about it. The purchasing of *Aluffe* coincided with the dust settling after one decidedly grim hiatus. Keeping my head down and getting a semblance of order together was the correct path to choose but 3 years on my natural inclination to shake things up was clearly beginning to kick in big time. How considerate it was, then, of nature to push the inevitable along by entering the mix at 30 knots one otherwise fine September afternoon in 2005.

Taking a late summer holiday on *Aluffe* Jacqui and I were storm bound for a few days in Plymouth. Twiddling our fingers in an expensive marina was not on our planned agenda. Keen to keep moving, we took advantage of a break in the weather to make the 20 mile trip to Salcombe. The weather was fine when we departed although the wind was expected to rise gradually as the day wore on but not beyond a manageable rate. With a moderate breeze from the south-west we threw all the sails up and set off, only partially noting the dark band of cloud way off in the distance. It didn't stay there for long because the band of weather tracked across the sky as if it had something really very important to do elsewhere. It swept over us within a couple of hours of our departure. With a rising onshore wind and a building sea we found ourselves in an unfavourable position. If a problem had arisen with the boat then we could have been in trouble. But in the absence of any problem I was more inclined to giggle as *Aluffe* flew in the face of it all.

At first I occupied myself with various calculations that began to fire through my head in relation to our situation. 'How fast are we travelling? How fast is the wind travelling? How far is it to Salcombe? Are we going to make it without the assistance of the coastguard?' It is proof of a misguided personal insecurity that my main concern was that Jacqui might crack in the face of rising waves and high winds, demanding that we call for help. I feared the apparent ignominy of requiring assistance above that of actually being caught out in dangerous conditions unprepared. Pride comes before a fall, they say, but thankfully there was no fall for I had the good fortune of being in the company of a Jacqui that day who was of a mind to instruct me to tie her to the mast if things took a turn for the worse or if she began to cause trouble. We were also fortunate to be on board a feisty *Aluffe* in the mood to show some character.

Force 7 would normally prompt the reduction of sail on a smaller boat long in advance of its arrival. However, a combination of surprise, prevarication, and enjoyment meant that when the wind was reaching its peak we were still carrying a full mainsail and large genoa. Not surprisingly we were whipping along as a result, with every other wave sending the boat off on a surf. The helm was light and responsive, giving all the exhilarating feedback that I required to make me feel very jolly. The genoa did come down towards the end but to exaggerate how precisely *Aluffe* dealt with the conditions is not possible. There was never a need to tie Jacqui to the mast because things never took a turn for the worse and deep down I think she enjoyed herself. This was largely due to the design and capabilities of *Aluffe*. If seeds of adventure had been sown in seasons past, they were effectively blooming out of control after our blustery arrival in Salcombe.

With the final piece of evidence being laid before me, the final proof that *Aluffe* was the vehicle in which I would answer a call of nature, there was need for a short pause while I considered the new direction in which my life was going to flow. Which direction exactly was still not known to me but clearly a boundary had been crossed and there was no immediate case for retracing my steps. I am not entirely gung-ho in my ways, however, and sorting out all those stumbling blocks so much in evidence only a short while before remained a necessary task.

Issues concerning the boat's suitability had been categorically quashed and work would solve itself with the completion of a contract at the end of the following year. A very handy full stop in that department had been provided. This would give me ample time to create an itinerary and ensure the boat was up to speed for a journey that had no burning need to end. There was still the consideration of money, always important, but already I could see that any departure would not be for at least a year giving me time to fiddle that one and put something aside for the trip itself. Going in *Aluffe* with its limited comforts down below meant I already felt I would be heading somewhere warm and in those climates it is possible to live on considerably less. Of course preparing the boat was going to cost, but surely the price is worth paying if something is worth having? Going was far more important than the monetary cost. In fact the only conundrum that was not easy to solve or address was that of my relationship.

Jacqui and I both enjoy sailing, but the sport has many facets. In fairness our interests were not mutual and might as well have occupied different ends of the spectrum at the time. Far more at ease with a pleasant day's sail along the coast with mild offshore winds, Jacqui was never going to be a big fan of overnighters and more in *Aluffe*. It had been my mistake to involve her in the infamous Channel crossing where she felt out of her depth. Putting her off the longer passages was unfair of me, although I suspect there would be a positive correlation between the size of boat and the length of trip she would be prepared to take. *Aluffe*, however, was the boat in which I would be going. For that reason and for Jacqui's understandable hesitancy towards dropping everything on my behalf, meant that we were in for an awkward discussion.

"Jacqui, I really think I am going to take *Aluffe* on a big trip, possibly around the North Atlantic." I ventured.

"Ok." The ball is still in your court, she might have added.

"If I go it will take at least 7 months for me to get around."

"I think that is a great idea and you should definitely go. A 7 month break from you will do me the world of good. I'm looking forward to it already."

Well, quite. Anything to oblige.

Chapter 3
Blood, sweat and Sikaflex

What great scheme has ever run seamlessly through each stage of its intended course? What grand plan has ever been achieved without so much as a tremor of the unexpected disturbing the minutiae of theoretical perfection? I'm no genius but would hazard a guess at none. Not only do I not believe that it has ever occurred but I do not believe that it could occur. Statistically I am sure it can be proved possible but in a world of such varying degrees, reality is the factor that will surely cock-up every well laid plan every time.

In this regard I was at an advantage with my great scheme because, short of a general concept and a wad of enthusiasm, I was woefully lacking in the wherewithal that might enable me to make it happen. There was a long way to go before calling it great because I did not even know where I was supposed to be heading. There was simply no plan in the early days. It had not escaped my notice that I would shortly be sanctioning the loss of a lot of cash. Becoming very well acquainted with the innards of my tool box was also to be anticipated but the thought of any well-laid plans being thrown off course by an unforeseen googly bothered me not the slightest. I was, however, pretty pissed off when *Aluffe* broke free of her mooring and ran ashore unexpectedly.

The strong winds that drove us towards Salcombe, the same ones that finally opened my eyes to the possibility of great adventure in *Aluffe*, heralded the arrival of even stronger winds. From the middle of September, through October, and well into November, low pressure systems plundered their way across the Atlantic before roughing up the likes of the Cornish. No-one suggested it was personal but as front after front powered through with the accompanying dark skies and rain, the option to offer a human sacrifice in appeasement seemed ever more attractive.

The major drawback for me was not being able to transfer *Aluffe* from her summer mooring in Falmouth to St Winnows, near Fowey further east along the coast, where she was kept over the winter months on a diversified farm. Boats regularly sail in rough and windy conditions similar to those encountered along the south coast that autumn. It is not uncommon for conditions to be even worse and still hardy vessels and crew bash their way on to chosen destinations. It is not often, however, that a skipper will voluntarily take their boat out of an excellent and sheltered anchorage like Falmouth into a sea being whipped up by onshore winds exceeding 40 knots. It was never my intention to disturb the figures surrounding that fact and so delayed again and again the necessary end of season trip to Fowey.

I am a firm believer in taking to bed with plenty of drugs in the event of illness. Sympathy is not discouraged but, in the main, self pity will suffice until any deadly ailment has been suppressed. When I was at school and the regular strains of debilitating flu swept through during the winter months, it would be seen as a sign of great weakness by my contemporaries and I if we succumbed and retreated to the comforts of our beds. Instead we dragged ourselves stoically to our lessons, and spluttered our way out to the sports pitches. It was in those heady days that I was first introduced to tutorials and 7-aside rugby such was the depletion in pupil numbers. We could never hope to maintain an intake of liquids that rivalled the waterfalls of snot gushing from our chapped red noses but crumble we did not. Sometimes the school would lie besieged for weeks as epidemics laid waste to our numbers before catching hold in another and then being past back again via someone's brother or sister at another school. Throughout it all we would force ourselves on until our strength finally yielded as our health had done a long time before. To this day I do not understand why our teachers permitted these absurd acts of pre-pubescent machismo. During my university days I eventually struck on the idea that giving up straight away was probably a better course of action. I was of the same opinion when I contracted what must have been a rare and nasty strain of life-threatening flu at the end of those blustery

October days and so headed to bed with plenty of drugs to sustain me. Informed by the Falmouth Harbour Commissioner that *Aluffe* had taken it upon herself to attempt an amphibious landing on the Cornish coast, however, forced me to draw on my schoolboy experiences and make an effort. Even in the absence of a plan a free roaming boat was definitely not right.

The immediate problem of *Aluffe* bumping about in the small harbour at Flushing, a small village on the northern side of Falmouth Harbour, was quickly solved. It was apparent that the wind wrestling with *Aluffe* had placed a huge strain on the mooring lines and they had parted overnight. It was an observant commuter working in the Harbour Commissioner's office who noticed that *Aluffe* was not only new to the Flushing quay but wasn't actually tied to it either. Miraculously she had drifted through a selection of moored boats and found the truest of routes into the tiny harbour where she became cosseted by the warps of a group of fishing boats. Had the wind been a few points to the west everything could have been so different. *Aluffe* would have probably wended her way through the moorings as before but then been pressed onto a rocky shoreline doing unthinkable damage. Despite the hindrance of a grave illness I manfully organised her recovery and let everyone know that luck had been on my side and the show was still on.

My relative good humour was marginally spoilt when I received a week later a letter from another boat owner requesting my insurance details as a result of the 'regrettable incident' when *Aluffe* took his boat off its mooring. Further to an inspection by experts, he added, his boat had suffered some damage and he would be claiming £3194.90 to cover the repairs.

That was not good news. Worse, however, was that any insurance details I could have given my claimant would have been of little value if, as they surely would, my insurers had pointed out the policy was null and void by virtue of the incident taking place on 1st November. In an attempt to keep my premiums down the arrangement was to take *Aluffe* out of the water and any harms way by the end of each summer season. That would be 31st October. With the steady stream of storms delaying me from keeping my end of the bargain the insurance company, understandably, saw a legitimate way out and declined to bail me out of my predicament.

Parting with that money would have been a serious inconvenience but it would have been paid had it not been for 2 factors in my favour.

The first was that old chestnut, a lack of evidence. The incident definitely happened overnight but there was nothing to suggest *Aluffe* and the other boat did not break free separately and arrive in Flushing of their own accords before becoming acquainted. Whilst *Aluffe* may have caused some damage, she was not at fault unless she had indeed pulled the other boat off the mooring and there was no proof to indicate this was the case. I wrote and explained this to the damaged boat's owner along with the message from my insurers. What I did not say in the letter, just managing to hold back, was that he was a liar.

The second factor in my favour related to the extent of damage to his boat when not a scratch could be found on *Aluffe*. I checked out his boat in the yard which had supplied the estimate of works and, suffice to say, the job list was generous. It was, arguably, an obvious con for my claimant to try but I do blame him. No-one died or lost their shirt and he didn't get away with it but such activity is annoying and unhelpful, acting to the detriment of a happy world. I assume he knows this because I never heard from the git again.

Eventually *Aluffe* was lifted out at St Winnows without further mishap and the business of pulling the project together began in earnest. Initially a scatter gun approach was taken buying and collecting random pieces of kit that seemed relevant. Whilst I did not commit anything to paper at first a mental list was generated and sporadic amendments were made with a liberal use of the internet. During one trawl of the marine service directories I happened across a second-hand Navic wind vane self-steering gear. As is the way of spontaneous and successful retail it was conveniently close and I whipped over to look, returning home £650 lighter in the pocket. In my possession was a piece of equipment that transforms the art of solo sailing by controlling the helm, thereby allowing the skipper to attend to other aspects of the boat. It also signified a serious step up in my organisation and planning.

I got very excited with the acquisition of the Navic, setting it up inconveniently in the house and marvelling at its ability to hold a boat on the perfect course in relation to the wind without the interference of the skipper. This prompted me to think more about to where it was exactly that the Navic was expected to steer *Aluffe*. I had previously referred in my discussions with Jacqui to the idea of a North Atlantic circuit, but such references had been vague at best. Carefully studying a chart it was not long, however, before a route from the UK to the Canaries had been more seriously sketched. From the Canaries I had an interest in the longer passage direct to Barbados to see how I might react to 3 weeks or more on my own. The opportunity to be alone for any length of time is rare in this world and I didn't want a deviation to the Cape Verde Islands to dilute that. There are a number of routes back to the UK from the Caribbean and it was not then confirmed which islands I intended to visit on the return journey, but the UK was to be the target destination.

It is well known that to cross the Atlantic east-west by my chosen route it is best done not before November and no later than March if one is to tap into the advantageous trade winds. Coming back along a more northern route a departure from the Caribbean during May is traditional, thereby avoiding the early tropical storms rushing through the area. I was committed to seeing out my work contract until the end of 2006 which posed a problem. Plugging south from the UK in mid winter sets a boat directly up against any of the storms that are commonly found in the Western Approaches to the Channel and further on in the Bay of Biscay. It is also cold. Even if that was not enough of a deterrent the Canaries are some 1700 miles away which would be a fair old slog in a small boat like *Aluffe*. There would not be the time for many or any long stopovers in ports along the way if the Caribbean was to be fully enjoyed. Even if *Aluffe* held together without any complications the chances of me arriving fresh in the Canaries and raring to embark on a 3 to 4 week passage across the Atlantic would have been slim. What to do? The simple answer was to get the boat as far south and beyond the Bay of Biscay as possible during my summer holidays, leaving her in the care of our Continental cousins, before returning in January to continue the journey. If I managed to get far enough south I would have the need for only a small weather window in which to get safely into warmer and more predictable climes.

With the plan taking shape around some notable geographical points and time lines it was easier to prioritise an approach that would enable me to even imagine completing all the preparations that were necessary if a successful trip was to be achieved at all. Prior to this point it had been all too easy to talk broadly about fixing the boat up while enjoying the notion of expansive oceans, sunsets and beaches, but at that stage they were merely glossy distractions. Dipping into the important detail caused immediate brain meltdown as the enormity of the task quickly became overwhelming. Having established a desire to get below the Bay before the close of the British summer the need to have *Aluffe* dressed and ready for 'sea trials' with a couple of months to spare was clear to see. Such a need could have created its own panic. Whereas I had originally envisaged having over a year to prepare *Aluffe*, what with the delays getting her ashore and an earlier departure from the UK this time had been slashed to 6 months. Surprisingly, avoiding the terminal wobble that offered itself to me, I found myself very excited at this prospect. The intensity of my life took a serious turn for the greater and I relished the sense of day-to-day purpose that had to be embraced, balancing boat stuff with work and domestics. The target of getting *Aluffe* prepared and in the water by the end of May became a mandatory element of each structured day.

It is very easy to view a goal and consider the way to get to it in an almost off-hand way. To do so ignores the detail of each element and stage required to achieve that goal. It is true that in practice not all the stages of a plan turn out to be as relevant as they might have been thought to be at the outset. However, to ignore the importance of each element in the first instance is akin to tying a hand behind one's back. To underestimate how much time each element will take is to shoot your foot off.

Having grasped the need for proper planning I duly considered all that had to be done before launching in May. There was no question that I was to renew the standing and running rigging. Likewise the windows would be replaced and the inboard engine overhauled. Or would it? Maybe I would replace it with a modern version or cut a hole in the cockpit suitable for an outboard engine? Whatever, I would come back to that. Replacing the electrics was essential as was fitting the Navic. The sails were workable but a new main was required and, on principle, *Aluffe* would be going no-where without a spinnaker on board. The interior of the boat was sound but a modicum of shoring-up of the minor locker partitions would be necessary along with a redesign of the galley and navigation station. Some new deck fittings would be required and the compass had to be installed. The sail handling systems were adequate but a few alterations at some point would improve them as well.

On the whole, there existed a clear list of things to do. A sound order in which these things had to be done was also in evidence. It is my firm belief that the initial plan of refit was so to the point that had it worked *Aluffe* would have been lacking nothing by the time of her launch at the end of May. But it didn't work. It didn't work because I had inaccurately factored in, if at all, mistakes, the need to learn, and even some incompetence.

Leaving the old windows with a glazing firm to cut new ones I concentrated in January on dropping the mast and detaching the old rigging to be measured for a new set. Only a short wait for a small fitting delayed the delivery of that but, courtesy of my decision to make a quick alteration to the gooseneck (linking the mast to the boom) the mast was not ready to step until the middle of June. The windows were collected and fitted in the meantime, but not before the mistakes of the glazer had been rectified.

I had always intended to take on the majority of the work on the boat. Not only would it be cheaper but it would give me an excellent working knowledge of *Aluffe* and her systems. Should a breakage occur at sea, far better for me to be comfortable using the right tools in the right place than scratching my head forlornly. In so doing I discovered that *Aluffe* was not symmetrical. Not far off, but not. It meant that fitting the Navic, for example, did not involve a simple placement along the centre line because it was not obvious that the centre line was, in fact, in the centre. Measuring from what, logically, was the centre line meant the discovery that the port side was fractionally wider than that of the starboard.

Whilst the fitting of the Navic provided for a short burst of entertainment, setting the rig up accurately was a far more protracted affair. It went up quickly and was strong, but for a long time *Aluffe* sailed upwind appreciatively better on starboard tack than port. After an inordinate amount of tweaking at every stopover it was not until I reached the Caribbean island of Sint Maarten a year later that I was eventually satisfied.

Likewise, in making alterations to *Aluffe* I learnt that remarkably little on a boat can be bought off the shelf. Of course, hours of nerdy hardware fun can be had in any half decent chandlers. Shelf after shelf will carry plenty of widgets and gadgets that are standard across the marine industry. *Aluffe* carried many standard fittings of old on board although some needed replacing. Often a replacement would do the same job as the old but might require an adjustment at its anchor point. The incompatibility of things was aptly demonstrated when I set about my quick alteration to the gooseneck, discovering that the only way to do it properly was to fabricate my own design. It was always rewarding to analyse a problem and then designing a successful fix. The problem lay in the time they all took and the resulting tattered mess that was my plan.

The only option available to me before long was to ignore the cosmetic and concentrate on the practical. It is an excellent approach to list management, one I had attempted to uphold from the beginning but that had suffered from the onslaught of the irrelevant and the additional. I would periodically return home after another late evening on the boat bemoaning the process of making a step forward before being forced to retreat 2. Jacqui bore with it to a point but, understandably, made it clear that it was my idea, my adventure, and therefore should be my burden, and not before long either. Her support was always there, however, and I quite enjoyed the moments when, as I collapsed with my head in my hands, she would assume the role of dominatrix and facilitate a re-planning meeting involving long lines of post-it notes and stern tones demanding my concentration. I cannot deny that it was not only rewarding but quite alluring as well.

Gradually, more rapidly as spring arrived, the important tasks were knocked off. There was still a multitude of smaller 'nice' tasks, including the making of curtains, but by applying a harder, practical approach the likelihood of getting *Aluffe* in the water by the end of June became more possible to believe. May had been scrapped as a launch date back in February.

One merry-go-round of a problem was that of the engine. The original inboard Petters 6 horsepower diesel remained doing sterling service although it was beset with problems common in older marine engines. It dropped oil, squirted water, and refused to tick over slowly when careful manoeuvring was necessary but it was on the whole reliable. Not only was its role to push the boat along on demand but it also had to charge the starter battery and the deep-cycle domestic battery. At first it seemed sensible to get the engine overhauled but, being old and having been superseded by newer and more efficient models, there was a thought that there might be a better option. Not many Achilles 24's have inboards as a small outboard is suitable for pottering in and out of moorings and marina berths. It is possible to get outboards that can also charge batteries and I began to think it would be good to have a reliable, lighter outboard for my trip. The cost was not excessive but it would have involved cutting a special hole in the boat into which the engine would be placed when in operation. That hole, I quickly came to see, was going to cause me time, money and probably problems. Putting the outboard idea on hold, the search for a modern inboard began. This was successful but also highlighted that a new engine would be expensive and involve further restructuring of the engine-bay to cater for its different specification.

I was pondering my options when Paul, a local engineer, sidled over and pointed out his penchant for all things Petters, letting it slip that he had a garage full of old ones and spares. Spares, that is, that were no longer available off the shelf but with which he could recondition mine. Good as new. Special rates applied. I didn't know what the rates were in the first place so how special the ones being offered were remained unclear. I took Paul up on his pitch nonetheless and so, returning to my original idea, I dragged the engine out and left it with him. He gave it a new lease of life and duly returned it in good enough time but the whole process had taken 6 months and an inordinate amount of brain ache. The one element of the boat that bore comparison was the electrics.

I do not believe I am alone but electrics give me the shivers. It is the knowledge that within the wires of any circuit there lies, or runs, buzzes, whatever one likes, some things called electrons. Such is their behaviour that if crossed they get very agitated very quickly and often very dangerously so. Tree surgery was my chosen profession for a while and contracts with power distribution companies were much sort after. They offered steady and reasonably well paid work. They also offered, less attractively, the opportunity to swing about in trees clearing branches growing too close to or around electric cables. The bigger high voltage lines were always shut down when work was being carried out but the smaller tributaries were commonly left on. Getting a tingle down the arm only happened to me once but that, and the knowledge that other climbers had not been so lucky, has always obscured my desire to understand electrical systems, preferring instead to seek sanctuary in ignorance. It is an odd thing, really, where one knows it to be so dangerous, understanding electrics might be considered advantageous. When it came, however, to refitting the simple electrical systems on board, I was very much in the dark hoping for a spark to go off in my head.

Eventually that spark did go off but it took the patience of more than one friend to painstakingly explain what I had, what I wanted and how to get it. For months I fretted and sweated over which bits were required and where to put them. I also applied myself to why and I think it was with the answering of that question that the bulb began to glow. With each iota of understanding gradually sinking in I approached *Aluffe* and her innards with a growing confidence to the point when, one momentous day, the wire clippers were pulled out in anger. It was a liberating feeling in many ways ripping out the old but far exceeded when I was eventually able to sit back and survey the mass of new cables running along the starboard side of the boat. Realising after the event that they all ran past the newly installed compass affecting its accuracy was a bad moment. But, brimming with new found knowledge and a maturing appreciation of the way of things, relaying them on the port side was within my stride. What made the process all the more interesting was the consequential need to rebuild the interior to cater for the new battery positions, swapping the galley over with the navigation station in the process. More problems, more jobs, more time, but always more learning.

As the weather improved and the evenings stretched out, longer hours were spent at the boat. On one occasion, after saying goodnight to friends who were staying with us I drove the 15 miles to the boat yard and did not return until gone 2 o'clock in the morning. This and other cases of extreme preparation did not endear me to Jacqui's favours. After the initial excitement at learning she would have 7 months to rattle about the house doing her own thing without the need to 'care' for me, the reality of being largely excluded from my big trip was causing a tension between us.

I had hoped that the whole trip might have been more of a joint effort in the same way a race team might have a support crew. This never came about, unfortunately, possibly because every aspect of the boat refit was new to me and I never really knew what was going to crop up next. My constant talk about the boat and endless journeys to it became too one dimensional for Jacqui.

There is generally an expectation amongst couples that their lives and the parts that make them up will be largely shared. Long periods of time apart, unless forced upon them by one or other's career, is uncommon if only because it indicates that their interests are not entirely compatible. The situation in which Jacqui and I found ourselves was uncommon, more so because it came about quite suddenly in the end. I did not have a history of shooting off for long periods to pursue one whim or another and so to do so then came as a surprise and denied us any real period of acclimatisation. Unfortunately, my desire to 'do something different' was linked to an activity that did not hold enough of an interest for Jacqui. Once bitten by the notion of the trip I would have found it nearly impossible to back away. Thankfully, Jacqui did not try to push me into that corner. Perhaps she should have done and I should have removed the blinkers because for a long while over the spring and into the summer we bumped along in a way that neither of us would claim to have been much more than satisfactory.

The good times surrounding the launch eventually came in mid-July. The run up to the occasion was marred only by an unfathomable mistake by the sailmaker who had been asked to adjust a second-hand mainsail to fit *Aluffe's* rig. A simple enough operation which, unfortunately, outwitted him. How none of us really worked out but the sail was rendered tiny, misshaped and useless, prompting a further large cheque to be paid in advance of a brand new one being delivered. This was to be after the launch and so I busied myself refitting an old mainsail and ungenerously barking orders at friends generously offering their services.

It had been a good summer and most of the necessary jobs had been completed but a lengthy list of 'non-essentials' was still to be worked through. The few weeks that remained before I set off for my trip south did not see a drop in activity and I was often to be seen paddling out to *Aluffe* on her mooring with a box of parts and a bag of tools. A solar panel to provide power was screwed on and connected, and the night before departing I clambered up the mast in the dark to make adjustments to the masthead lights. Swaying gently at the top of the mast I looked around me at the other yachts resting peacefully on their moorings, silhouetted by the lights of Falmouth. The calm they exuded contrasted so exactly with my efforts. There was no escaping how much time, energy, and emotion was involved in getting everything ready. It could have, and nearly did on a couple of occasions, become too much of a burden in amongst the grind of work and my efforts to pull something close to my weight at home. And yet the moments of doubt were unmentionably rare as the adrenalin and drive flowed unchecked for months. I had sunk my teeth well and truly into the project and only a fool in my position would have given it up.

The decision had been taken to try and reach Nazare, approximately half way down Portugal between Lisbon and Porto. Exactly how long it would take depended, of course, on the disposition of the weather but I believed *Aluffe* would be capable of nearly 100 miles a day. The overall distance was 900 miles and so there would be ample time in theory in my 2 week holiday to get there and make arrangements for her prolonged stay. Last minute panics included a trip round the supermarket with Jacqui who then packed away set meals for each day. The good weather towards the end of August had begun to depreciate and I feared that I might be prevented from leaving by strong winds. In the end, however, an encouraging Force 6 from the north-west was to be my companion out of Falmouth and into the Channel.

Threading my way through the moorings in Falmouth Harbour I allowed myself a moment of emotion and even a tear in the eye. It was not because Jacqui was standing alone on the quay, waving me off. There was friction between us then but we both realised that a 2 week break would be a welcome rest and I looked forward to getting back to smooth over the cracks in our relationship. My emotion came with the realisation that I was really off. At last, on 26th August, I was setting sail in *Aluffe*, my little boat, and heading out into the big sea, just as I had intended. The effort had been non-stop over the past 7 months and finally the rewards were being reaped. With all of that behind me I felt I had really achieved something already. My goal was ultimately to return to Cornwall via the Caribbean but departing was a hugely significant moment which did not pass me by. I was elated and beaming broadly as *Aluffe* left the coast behind to the north. Looking ahead I saw only the sea.

Vertigo is not a problem to me as I have no fear of heights. Climbing trees for a living in my twenties I had no qualms about clambering around the largest oak and beech trees in amongst their top most branches. Sometimes the trees would sway wildly in the wind but I was never bothered. My attitude was always that if I could climb along a branch 3 metres off the ground, there was no reason why I could not do the same 30 metres further up. Likewise I used to rock climb. Not a lot, but enough to support the evidence suggested by my tree climbing that heights were for me something more to relish than fear. What I did fear, very much in fact, was letting go. The consequences of doing that did not excite me at all and perhaps explained why I possessed an almost limpet like quality to my aerial activities.

Letting go meant a fall and a fall meant a fast descent over which I could claim no control. I am rubbish at cliff jumping for the same reason. After the jump there is the fall and the inability to slow down should the desire present itself. The trick was, therefore, to stay attached. Such a fear did not, however, stop me from attempting, at 111 metres, the highest known commercial bungee jump in the world over the River Zambezi in the mid-nineties on a trip to Zimbabwe.

I recall puffing myself up with positive mantras and becoming very excitable, talking gibberish to all and sundry whilst the elastic band was tied to my legs. I watched as others before me threw themselves off the bridge and descended with arms spread in perfect swallow dives. I too threw myself off the bridge and experienced a burst of euphoria at having made the jump, at having overcome in that instant my fear of letting go. That burst of euphoria turned to utter panic a fraction of a second later as I grasped to where it was I had jumped, and that I had not succeeded at all in overcoming my doubts about falling. Dropping like a stone I screamed vivid obscenities as my arms flailed wildly. Interestingly, it was not a mind numbing terror that gripped me. I managed to calculate, in the few moments available to me at reaching the limit of my descent before being pinged back towards my recent point of departure, that with an 80 percent recoil I was soon to be subjected to the delights of possibly the second highest commercial bungee jump in the world. Tackling my fear of letting go was one thing but accepting where I ended up was another altogether.

As *Aluffe* was driven away from the Lizard and the known waters surrounding Cornwall, I absorbed that moment of triumph whilst appreciating that I was entering into a place in which I had barely any experience. The hard bit had been done but facing me then was the unknown. The big open sea was ahead and excitement mixed awkwardly with apprehension.

Chapter 4
An unfamiliar world

It felt unnatural to find myself alone at sea and beyond the sight of land for the first time. Removed from the countless reference points that were familiar to me onshore, all those that induced a sense of belonging and subsequent calm, placed me in a new territory and in need of wising up to the unfamiliar surroundings.

With the sea stretching out for miles all around to an unbroken horizon I was acutely aware that my world, all that was known to me and all to which I could immediately associate, had shrunk confusingly into a 24 foot sailing boat. Fortunately I had none of the feelings of vulnerability that can affect some sailors who are freaked out by the mass of water below the keel of their boats and the absence of a safe haven. *Aluffe* actually seemed plenty big enough but, without any company on board, I was denied the immediate stimulation of conversation and also the comfort that any troubles encountered could be shared. The natural order of things was distorted in the first few days while I tried to settle into a routine and adapt to the strange rhythms influencing our progress.

For all the excitement of leaving, however, there was a need to pace the rate at which I acknowledged the differences if I was not to become overwhelmed. To temper my emotions and instil a basis of composure I concentrated on sailing the boat, a familiar activity, and making sure we were going in the right direction.

There was certainly no sense of physical calm or stillness as *Aluffe* was buffeted by a short sea and persistent winds. The boat presented only a small target but waves regularly caught her with a sharp smack on the bow sending bursts of salty spray down her length and over me at the stern. In nervous overdrive I was in and out of the cabin keeping track of my position far more than was necessary. I drove for long periods gaining comfort from having some control in this new and wet mix. Only gradually, as the miles dropped behind, was the Navic left in control.

Adrenalin was fuelling me in the main but I knew that regular rest, food and drink were crucial if I was to keep myself together, particularly in light of the squally weather that was harrying *Aluffe* south. Unfortunately, sea sickness took hold early meaning I had 2 fewer things to address which could act as reminders of the normal way of things. With the novelty of the situation absorbing so much of my attention rest was something that came in fits and starts. It occurred as and when my need to sleep coincided with me feeling well enough to get out of my damp sailing gear, and fall onto my makeshift bed on the floor of the cabin, before a rising nausea forced me to retch hopelessly on an empty stomach.

My mind was constantly on the go trying to make sense of the new environment. It was not that the sea was unfamiliar or that the wind was blowing any differently to what I might have experienced in the past but, more used to spending hours at sea, there was a struggle initially to fully understand their role and relevance over the course of days. If the waves were doing one thing at a certain point what would they be doing at the next? How would those dark clouds in the distance affect my progress? We covered 200 miles in the first 48 hours, was that good? Was it important? All these questions joined others, including those relating to the motion of the boat and the sounds of the sea, in my bid to establish a sense of order. With no-one else on board it was down to me, not necessarily to answer them all, but to at least assess their relative value.

In the life I had temporarily left behind on land thousands of bits of stuff intruded on my daily activity at all the levels of my conscious. Peripheral motion, subtle touches, and snippets of overheard conversation, to name only 3, each register to some degree. The vast majority are irrelevant but they still occupy the mind which has to process and act upon them accordingly. In contrast, sailing aboard *Aluffe* greatly reduced the number of stimuli acting on me. Without the complexity of people and land providing distractions I thought of only a few but very relevant issues, namely; condition of the boat, condition of me, sea state, weather, position, food, and sleep. It was not, however, a case of being bored and having nothing to do for I thought of them all the time. Whilst my world had effectively shrunk and my mind become less crowded life was far from being less intense. In fact, everything I thought and did increased dramatically in importance.

This focusing of the mind out of necessity was very liberating. Everything I did about the boat had definite purpose in the attempt to get *Aluffe* from Falmouth to Nazare. I enjoyed the demands of the simple tasks such as adjusting the sails, rocking my body in tune with the motion of the boat, and ducking the spray to remain dry. Devoid of any complicating side issues and distractions, their significance was far greater on board. It was a long way from being comfortable in those first 3 days out of Falmouth but it was refreshing and energising nonetheless. The change in my circumstances was stark and my apparent ability to adapt was gratifying.

I recalled a friend, a gnarly and free thinking woodsman, promoting the virtues of 'living on the edge'.

"It's where things happen," he had said.

I felt I was living on my edge by tackling the trip. It had taken me away from the comfort zone of work and the security of the life I had created on land and placed me in a small wet boat on the edge of an ocean. In so doing I was extracting bucket loads of satisfaction by facing all manner of discomforts in a way that I could never have imagined possible otherwise. I was being tested at a fundamental level. The gale was a fantastic eye-opener which pushed me through a new experience and to a higher level of seamanship. My woody friend was quite correct and 'Live on the edge, it's where things happen' became something of a mantra for the duration of the trip. Without a willingness to peak over the fence from time to time, there is the danger that many potentially edifying moments will pass by unfulfilled. Granted it cannot be for everyone and there are costs but proof of its value came when I pottered past an extraordinarily large whale in the aftermath of the gale.

By 'extraordinarily large whale' I mean the bit that was visible. The gale had gradually faded away with the day and moving towards a windless evening *Aluffe* chugged gently through a flat sea. Gazing absentmindedly towards the horizon my eyes were caught by the sudden appearance of a spout of water. The small fountain dissipated slowly into a haze and was gone.

'Whale,' my brain clunked out the answer.

As my eyes focussed in on the spot 150 metres to starboard I caught sight of a small fin being conveyed under the surface by an arched black mass of something.

"Whale," I confirmed out loud.

Just knowing that there was a large mammal in the vicinity was enough for me to feel that same sense of wonderment about which so many witnesses write when in the company of whales. I was also a little nervous thinking that maybe this whale was leading a calf. Being close with an engine running might threaten her.

'In fact,' I thought, 'where is she?'

On demand the answer appeared 50 metres to my stern. What I saw was extraordinarily large but the broad black back that rolled slowly towards me was attached to something enormous. I cannot give an accurate figure of how big the solitary whale was but without a doubt it was significantly more than twice the length of *Aluffe* at nearly 50 feet. I later discovered that it was probably a fin whale, the second largest mammal in the world. The sighting, never to be repeated, was magnificent. If a Japanese research vessel had passed by at that moment I would have rammed it without hesitation.

It was not just the physical size that was so awe inspiring, after all most of the whale's bulk was below the water and out of sight. There was, in addition, an unmistakable aura of belonging generated with its presence. That whale had its reference points and it showed. The ease with which it so gracefully moved its bulk through the water highlighted on whose patch I was treading. It gave me the impression that *Aluffe* was a desperately insignificant speck of a boat in which to place my trust and that I was very definitely not in the environment to which I was born. It was a similar feeling to that experienced when watching lions and rhino in their natural habitats. The same can be said of all fauna that have evolved over millennia to be perfectly suited to their natural environment. Observing these animals and seeing their movements up close, their muscles rippling, noses sniffing the air, has a far greater impact in the wild than in a zoo. Looking up from a car at a bull elephant towering above has the same affect. Humans clearly have the ascendancy in the natural world through not only their ability to adapt to environments but also through an ability to adapt environments to their needs. However, there is something offensive about that level of dominance which comes from an endless desire to extend boundaries, or live on the edge. It has been the way of the world, I suppose, and deep respect is all I could offer the whale in return for extending my boundary across its natural borders without invitation.

Studying the many birds that accompanied me was captivating. They went about their business with a precision in flight that was nothing if not impressive. Petrels seemed just too small to be allowed out so far from land but there they were skimming over the surface unconcerned by all the weather conditions. During the course of the gale a couple were spotted sitting it out unperturbed, rising and falling with the waves. I was heartened by their presence which was not dissimilar to that of *Aluffe's* on the big sea.

Shearwaters were plentiful and notable for their unexpected grace. Not an entirely attractive bird, there is something functional about their design and appearance. They have the look of something that could be smartened up around the edges but I would not suppose they actually need any evolutionary tinkering. Their ability to fly was spectacular. Using the lift generated off the front of a wave they would drift low over the water searching for food before rising in a gentle loop and dropping to one in arrears. Any wave was enough to give them lift, no matter how small, it seemed. In the more choppy conditions they remained drawn to the wave fronts, mere fractions of millimetres from the surface. Watching their wing tips it was possible to see them flicker over each individual ripple. It was tempting to think that it was a deliberate flexing of the tips on the part of the shearwaters but I suspect it had more to do with the small amounts of upward pressure affecting the lightweight feathers.

Being such accomplished fliers, and they are not alone in this I believe, some would sleep, or at least doze, in flight. That is kind of clever and would be very efficient if it was necessary to get somewhere far off in a hurry, but it does have its complications. There are 2 shearwaters who can testify to the difficulties posed by small sailing boats appearing unannounced at night. My dog can see in the dark and I imagine many animals can do the same. Perhaps they can but if a bird, a shearwater even, is asleep in flight I guess their ability to see objects moving in the dark will not be improved.

Supporting this theory are the 2 occasions when I was jolted from my sleep with the abrupt arrival of a shearwater crashing into the rigging before it tumbled to the deck. In fact one didn't make it down from the rigging choosing instead to loudly straddle the spreaders. It didn't look comfortable and once it had woken up, sussing out its predicament, it swiftly departed back into the night with some indignant squawking. The one that fell to the deck, I fear, got short shrift from me. Startled by its sudden appearance I got all defensive and bellowed at it to 'get off my ship!' The poor bird will never claim it to have been a positive episode in its life as it then flapped about getting caught up in some loose lines and a sail on the foredeck before flopping over the side for a dunking. Oops.

The first 4 days from Falmouth had been exciting and challenging with no small degree of discomfort thrown in for good measure. Conditions were always going to improve and so they did once the gale had made its point. The wind dropped off and the sun made more regular and longer appearances. I was able to have a decent wash and hang my clothes out to dry on the guardrails. The calming of the weather reflected the state of my own emotions. It was gratifying to have dealt well enough with the hectic nature of the past days and my stomach rewarded me by permitting the much needed intake of food and drink. Slowly I managed the dietary adjustment from a daily intake of zero to considerably more.

The carefully packed food bags that Jacqui had provided were soon in disarray. Every bag, supposedly one for each day, contained a selection of 3 main meals in the company of a range of snacks and treats. The arrangements made complete sense before departure but they did not translate well onto *Aluffe* in practice. As a solo sailor anything and everything that needed to be done on board had to be done by me. This included the preparation and cooking of food, not forgetting the clearing up afterwards. The demands of sailing a boat are not subject to strict itineraries and schedules. If the weather picks up at daybreak and a sail needs changing then it is breakfast that takes second place. With the spontaneity of this regime so new to me I quickly came to realise that I could not be doing with all the bother surrounding the issue of food. What can be such a pleasurable activity when the time is available and the conditions suit the company, can also be reduced to a functional refuelling stop when necessity demands. On the trip to Portugal I was not in a mood to express myself in the culinary department. Subsequently, a single stop approach was adopted in the evening when one large hot meal was cooked to supplement the snacks consumed as and when they were wanted throughout the rest of the day. That attitude to food worked well on the first leg when I was occupied in absorbing all of that which was new and different. On later legs my nutritional demands changed as I became more accustomed and appreciative of life at sea.

Having successfully cracked the Bay of Biscay it was necessary for me to continue south down the coast of Portugal in order to close on my chosen destination of Nazare. Before the coast could be reached, however, there was a need to head east as *Aluffe* was placed well to the west of Cape Finisterre off Spain and also the traffic separation scheme situated in that area. Cape Finisterre is one of those headlands around which many ships of all shapes and sizes carrying an equally varied range of cargoes travel. It is a sad fact that too many ships have in the course of history suffered from faulty navigation, mechanical failure, and/or bad weather. The price to pay has all too often been the loss of ship, cargo and life on rocky shores. To reduce the risk associated with passing around Cape Finisterre and other similarly exposed headlands traffic separation schemes operate. Large commercial vessels are instructed to follow designated routes thereby reducing the chances of running into land or another ship.

It would be nice to believe that these schemes are infallible, that every ship in areas where they exist is dedicated to abiding by the rules. They are excellent maritime developments and appeal to every scrap of logic. Unfortunately, such a common sense and self regulated approach to marshalling traffic does not tick everyone's box. In truth, the schemes work in the main but there is still evidence of ships going the wrong way up or down a lane. I was surprised by the appearance of 2 tankers on separate occasions heading towards the scheme off Cape Finisterre which would set them on courses contrary to the flow of traffic and the spirit of the rule book. With trawlers and other fishing vessels allowed to operate within them traffic separation schemes do not engender the feeling of security which must surely have been a significant part of their reason for being.

An associated problem lies in the fact that they are only situated in localised hot spot areas and can give a false sense of security to boats sailing outside their limits. A boat travelling south from France or Britain towards the Mediterranean out of the Cape Finisterre scheme will continue in a straight line to the next one rounding Cabo Raso. From there it will take the shortest route to the next scheme, clipping Cabo de Sao Vicente before bearing east through the Straits of Gibraltar. The point is that in between the separation schemes large, fast moving cargo ships do not simply evaporate. The threat of a collision with a small sailing boat remains the same anywhere along a shipping route, perhaps even more so because at least in the lanes ships are encouraged not to alter course.

The risk of being run down by a large ship was high on the list of concerns put to me by friends and family before I left. It is initially difficult to comprehend how, in such a vast and 'empty' space, one ship could possibly hit another at sea. There is reason for this disbelief in that ships mainly take direct or specified routes between their points of departure and arrival. It is quite easy to spot where these routes might be and note them on a chart. Sail in the large areas of sea that lie away from the main shipping routes connecting major commercial ports or bottle necks like the Straits of Gibraltar or Dover and the chances of bumping into something are greatly diminished. Crossing the routes, including those that run between, into and out of the traffic separation schemes, is the time for extra vigilance. I did not ignore this when it came to crossing east towards the Portuguese coast.

The day was cloudless and relatively still with only a light wind to help me. Seemingly all alone on the still blue waters, *Aluffe* slipped smoothly along while I stretched out in the cockpit, soaking up the sun. It was so quiet that I got to wondering if ships did in fact evaporate outside the separation schemes or perhaps there was a strike and no-one in the shipping industry was working. Munching on a light lunch of cheese and biscuits it became crystal clear that these were idle thoughts indeed, for there came bearing down on me an assortment of 7 ships spread out over a few miles. The idea that a lock gate was in operation within the separation scheme to the north crossed my mind. By this stage I was committed to crossing and waiting for them all to pass was likely to create some confusion amongst the officers on watch. Despite the light conditions we were under sail in order to conserve diesel but with the wind dropping further still I opted for more control and powered up the engine. The ships were travelling in 2 parallel lines about a mile apart meaning that my run across at right angles to the traffic had to be well judged. It wasn't and so, having nipped behind the stern of one tanker, I was forced to motor in the same direction as the others until a big enough gap presented itself, allowing *Aluffe* to zip through before the next ship growled past. With the southbound traffic left to my stern the traffic heading north was negotiated with ease as night fell. Pleased with my efforts I was able to get in a healthy feed before coming under torpedo attack.

Phosphorescence can be described as a vivid display of light that occurs at sea when certain non-metallic elements, or phosphors, are agitated. If present these elements momentarily illuminate and can give away the position of objects moving through the water. The moon was rising brightly into the night sky when I sighted the first torpedo (obviously!) streaking towards me. It past ahead of *Aluffe* but I lost sight of it as another followed and then another. Holding on to a semblance of rational thought I didn't immediately leap to the tiller and execute well rehearsed anti-submarine attack drills learnt in a misspent youth reading '*Commando*' comics. I tried instead to focus on why these torpedoes appeared to be veering wildly around the bow, even jumping out of the water on occasions.

Dolphins were the reason which, thankfully, lodged in my brain without too much delay. It was like watching an aquatic version of Tinkerbelle and friends leaving a trail of glittering stars behind in their play. The dolphins dived under *Aluffe* and sped along her side, criss-crossing their paths at the bow. Ahead I could see a luminous patch of shimmering green about 10 metres across. I was slower than my companions who quickly fathomed out the presence of a shoal of fish and darted off in its direction. Empty stomachs were obviously not pressing issues, however, because the meal was left largely to its own devices, moving en masse away from the boat which would have otherwise bisected the gathering.

It would not be for the last time on the trip that I wondered if *Aluffe* was too slow for the dolphins when they disappeared shortly afterwards. Perhaps if the bow wave was larger, and more water was being pushed aside by the hull, the dolphins would find the prospect of dancing around the bow more entertaining for longer. As it was I was left on my own to consider how best to reach my destination after an eventful day.

Before leaving I had estimated a 10 day passage but light winds and limited diesel had threatened an arrival within this time. Without a satellite phone the simple options for getting a message back to those expecting a call were limited. The start of Day 8 beckoned after a couple of days during which I toyed seriously with making for a closer port. I had become very content at sea and had barely noticed the days passing by, but was appreciative of the fact that it was not only a new adventure for me but also one for those close to me back at home to endure. Without contact for over a week it was unfair of me to be too casual about their concern on that first leg. With a little under 100 miles to go I should have been confident of making Nazare with time to spare their worries but the wind had been blowing weakly from the south too long for that. Scratching my head may be discovered one day to be a divine signal to the keepers of wind because in pondering the options the wind picked up from the north, building to a healthy Force 5 over night and continued for much of the next day. A fast and early arrival in Nazare was back on the cards. The only worry I had was not being able to see with the arrival of thick fog.

Strong winds and low visibility are common conditions along the Portuguese coast but the combination was a new experience for me. Without radar there was no way of knowing where any larger boats travelling up and down the coast might be. I had little faith in every ship sending out the relevant 'restricted visibility' sound signals. Other small boats were unlikely to have radar either and closer to shore we would encounter fishing buoys. These could wrap themselves around the prop and rudder, and the chances of spotting them were minimal. The conditions were poor and likely to remain so for some time which was difficult for me as tiredness was becoming a factor on the busy passage. As a test of my seamanship it was based more around my management skills than those technical.

Aluffe was comfortably rattling along at a high cruising speed, around 5.5 knots, but visibility was no more than 100 metres in any direction. Our course was gradually bringing us closer to land although initially we were 30 odd miles offshore when the wind began to fill in. Clearly there was a risk of a collision but how much of one and what I was to do about it were the questions that needed answering.

I opted pretty much to leave the sails up, maintain my course and speed, and go to bed. What might appear at first glance to be an example of poor judgement was, in fact, a calculated response in the face of a serious situation. What else was there to do? Calling for assistance was a non-starter without the existence of an emergency. Dropping sails until the fog lifted may have stopped me from running into something but *Aluffe* would still have been a target for another vessel on the move. I had a reasonable idea of where the inshore shipping lanes were and had to believe that *Aluffe*'s reflector in the rigging would be visible to any nearby radar operative. The main problems for me were the possibility of coming across a fishing vessel going about its business regardless of the conditions, and not being able to rest. The preceding week had been new and fascinating but it had also been physically and mentally demanding. One fact was certain and that was that I could not hope to remain awake indefinitely. I had to sleep and did so because gazing at fog for hours, anticipating the dreadful sight of a ship's bow ploughing remorselessly forward, was not only incredibly tiring but also did nothing for the state of my nerves. The fog was so thick my head was pointlessly spinning like a top trying to spot any movement within it. Taking courage from having worked through the options thoroughly I maintained a regular look-out but I also went to bed and played the odds.

Lying below while the boat is left to sail blindly on is not a concept that rests easily with many people. Indeed, *Rule 5* of the *International Regulations for Preventing Collisions at Sea* states 'Every vessel shall at all times maintain a proper look-out by sight and hearing.....' There was no question that my actions contravened the essence of the rule but to enforce it would mean the outlawing of single-handed sailing across the board and the end of such prestigious races as the Vendee Globe. That cannot be an acceptable option and so it remains for the solo skipper to exercise, rightly so, all due caution and proper judgement as appropriate. Even with plenty of that, however, barrelling through a blanket of fog while on deck or below remains a tricky prospect. I suspect it was partly in reference to those difficulties that many people questioned the sanity of my trip privately and openly. Since early on in the project it was not uncommon for me to explain my plans before being asked if I was mad. More often than not the question was overlooked altogether and I was simply told I was so.

Not unsurprisingly I did not agree with that mindset where madness might be seen as some form of mental disorder causing irrational and compulsive behaviour. It is ridiculous to think people believed I was actually mad in the literal sense but were more likely good naturedly alluding instead to an attitude and an act to which they would not subscribe. Personally, I drew considerable resolve from the historical records that supported the possibility of my trip. The knowledge that other solo sailors managed, some in Achilles 24's, bolstered my confidence to press on during the difficult days of preparation. As *Aluffe* and I pushed towards Nazare my trust in that same conviction grew as a direct result of having exercised proper judgement. Had *Aluffe* been cleaved in 2 by a cargo ship it would not have been for the sake of my madness. Stupidity, maybe, but not madness.

What was undoubtedly stupid was the belief on my part that the journey was almost over and that *Aluffe* and I would shortly be swept on the brisk wind right into the marina berth. Tying up alongside, I imagined, a glass of champagne would be thrust into my sweaty paw and the fishing town of Nazare would celebrate my triumphant arrival with a week long festival. Hardly. For starters the wind dropped off completely and granted me only the occasional zephyr. Unfortunately, the fuel situation was so poor by then I calculated there was no more than enough to manoeuvre within the confines of the port. And so we sat there, a mere 10 miles from Nazare, inching forward mainly by virtue of the current for 12 hours. Fortunately the fog had lifted and the stars made the night bearable but with daybreak we were still 6 miles short and travelling no faster. Land, though, was visible for the first time in 9 days. Its solidity and array of colour was at odds to all that I had become accustomed. Listening to the swell breaking on the yellow beaches was strange. It had become an unfamiliar sound and less of a reliable reference point.

I watched for a long time the bright white buildings of Nazare with their clay tiled roofs bathing in the same sun shared by the worshippers on the beach. Eventually, a matter of metres from the harbour entrance, I plucked up enough courage to start the engine. Pottering slowly towards the visitors' marina any remaining thoughts of mass celebrations dissolved with the realisation that I had arrived during the siesta, a time when the whole of southern Europe traditionally sleeps off a hearty lunch. The harbour control was obviously not missing out and could not be raised, leaving me to sort myself out.

I nestled into a small berth and stepped ashore after a shade over 9 days at sea alone, during which time nearly 900 miles had been covered. It was not a maritime feat worthy of national accolades, or festivals for that matter, but, given the ingredients, it was not a paltry achievement. It was massive for me. Despite having spent most of the trip frowning and gawping at the novelty factor I did not deny myself the pleasure of appreciating how I had adapted and learnt along the way. Heading to the showers for a much needed wash I deliberately walked just a little taller and more slowly. Savouring the moment of arrival was important and I felt the right to spend time reflecting on the passage had been earned. Frankly, I was chuffed to bits having made it but also at having enjoyed it so much.

The goal was always to try and sail *Aluffe* around the North Atlantic. There was, however, the proviso, in respect of my limited experience, that there would be no shame in backing out if difficulties were encountered or I ceased to enjoy the trip. What was easy to see almost immediately was that the big picture was simply too big to digest as a whole and my brain soon turned to mush when I tried. Viewing each stage as a separate entity reduced the pressure at every step of the way. Initially I had concentrated on preparing the boat and there had been a sequence of steps, if faltering, to follow. With that out of the way, I had to test myself and the boat at sea. That effort combined with the first leg. If the experience to Portugal had been a poor one I could, possibly even would, have amended the original goal. But it wasn't. In fact it had been a resounding success where *Aluffe* had performed exceptionally and I was left grinning from ear to ear.

The few days available to me before flying home were spent making alterations to *Aluffe*'s watertight locker spaces and packing up before lifting her out of the water. The marina was quite small but a varied collection of cruising folk and live-aboards made for easy company. There was no delay in meeting and greeting, with unsolicited offers of help following not far behind the invitation to 'come over for a beer'. In amongst the larger yachts *Aluffe* looked subtly precocious.

"So where've you come from, then?" Jim asked quizzically. He was from Northern Ireland and owned a 40 foot Hallberg-Rassey. He and his wife were planning on staying in Nazare over the winter with their 3 children.

I told him.

"Without stopping? Good on you. And where're you going from here?" he continued.

"Next stop the Canaries, and then Barbados. After that we'll see." I replied.

"On your own?" He looked me up and down.

"No room for anyone else, really." I shrugged.

"Fair play to you. You must be crazy."

Chapter 5
Flight to the Canaries

With the boat sitting 900 miles away on the hard in amongst an assortment of brightly coloured Portuguese fishing boats the main focus of my trip was no longer part of my daily life, as it had been for 8 months. This provided for a welcome break from the regular grind of preparation but it left me feeling slightly at a loss for practical things to do. It was a pleasure not to have to pull on my grotty jeans, stained with varnish and blood, once again but I missed the intensity they represented. To suggest, however, that I had nothing to do would be wrong. Having been rushed in the last days before setting out from Falmouth there was a long list of loose ends that needed my attention.

I had left the UK with only charts enough to get me to Portugal. There was still the need to buy those that would take me the whole way round the Atlantic. It was my intention to use paper charts rather than rely on an electronic chart plotter. The simple reasons behind this were the lack of power on board and my view that it was just not necessary. It wasn't so much a hankering to 'do it properly' but much more of a practical decision supported by a desire not to overcomplicate matters. I was also under the impression that a chart plotter would be expensive. Walking to my car under a pile of charts that covered all eventualities, however, it occurred to me that a modern, compact and lightweight chart plotter might also have been considerably cheaper.

'Never mind,' I thought 'Columbus, Slocum, and Knox-Johnston never used a chart plotter.' On that basis I also bought a sextant as back up to the basic GPS I already used. I had only a very basic understanding of the sextant but set myself a target to learn how to use it on the way around.

The idea of doing the trip was attractive for the opportunity it would give me to discover the extent of my capabilities in an uncompromising and honest environment. Very few people can claim to have control over the weather and I am not one of them, and the appeal of having to rely solely on my own wit to deal with whatever was to be thrown my way was a key part of the test. The reasoning behind not using a chart plotter had been one based on pragmatism but my original intention not to take a satellite phone was more guided by a romantic ideal. The notion of solitude and being at one with the sea in the spirit of Bernard Moitissier, the famous French sailor, guided my thinking in the first instance and I did not carry one to Portugal. The final days of that trip, however, had been troubled by an inability to make known my position and allay any fears at home. There was no danger to report and I could easily maintain the case that it was, therefore, not necessary to carry a satellite phone. But I realised in those days that I was getting heaps enough from the trip and the idea that I was cutting off others from the experience entirely was not adding to my adventure at all. Coming at it from a slightly different angle my parents obviously thought the same and after a bit of this and that to prevent me from losing face they persuaded me to accept a gift of a satellite phone.

"Just for emergencies," we all agreed.

There was a flurry of activity in the run up to the New Year as such chores as domestic paper work, finances and a supply of winter logs all demanded attention. It was not my intention to leave Jacqui with a mass of things to sort out on her own where we once shared the chores of domestic bliss. Excitement was riding high for me and even writing a Will was more of a thrill than something hinting at my possible demise. It hinted at the idea that I was doing something different. If I had ever thought death was a likely prospect I would never have left, but it was undeniable that the thought of things getting tricky was perversely alluring.

Eventually the time for farewells came around with the fading of the New Year celebrations. Noticeably the jovial 'are you mad?' comments had dwindled as the moment of departure drew closer. The realisation that I really was going, irrespective of my sanity, generated an uncomfortable air of sobriety. Jacqui by this time was less convinced by the supposed virtues of the impending period of separation and, with my blinkers attached, I missed how much my mother was worried. A lifetime in the navy had given my father an up close and personal understanding of how vicious the sea can be. It is not his style to make a fuss in a crisis but driving me to the airport his concern was barely disguised. I could not doubt his knowledge but to find out for myself was part of the deal. The moment for that was fast approaching, however, and, despite my relief at ending the waiting, I shared everyone's apprehension.

The actual act of getting back to Portugal was more a feat of weightlifting than a simple process of boarding a plane as I had managed to gather about me an impressive collection of essentials. It was agreed with Jacqui, who was due to join me in the Caribbean in March, that she would bring out some extra books and other kit but that still left me with an huge bag, bulging with charts, phones, books, and medical kits. Fortunately, dressed up like a Michelin man I and the bag successfully slipped on board without the payment of excess baggage.

The clock was ticking as far as I was concerned. The purpose of getting *Aluffe* to Nazare had been to get south of the Bay of Biscay and its winter storms leaving me with less of a leg to the Canary Islands, some 800 miles further south. It was from there that I would start my Atlantic crossing and my trip proper. Before that it was a matter of simply making tracks.

There was not much to do on *Aluffe* beyond carrying out the regular engine and rig checks, and painting on a layer of antifouling. She had fared well in my absence and within a couple of days of returning to the fishing port *Aluffe* was lifted from her cradle and put back on the water. Resting in the straps of the enormous boat lift, she looked pocket sized. A little daunted, I concentrated on the pulse of excitement running through me at the thought of the challenge ahead.

The main task left for me was to fill *Aluffe* with food and water. On the advice of Tony, one of the marina residents, I aimed to buy as much food as I could to last me for a fair chunk of my trip. Tony had lived in the Caribbean and Bermuda for many years and convinced me that I would have to re-mortgage my house soon enough if I insisted on not taking advantage of the low Portuguese prices.

Picking out the largest trolley available I marched around the supermarket grabbing armfuls of stock foods. Pasta, olive oil, wholemeal biscuits, porridge, longlife milk joined the many tins of vegetables and fruit. And squid. It was true that the prices in Portugal were low but so was the level of choice. Based on my experiences on the first leg I focused on buying the wherewithal for simple, single large meals with accompanying snacks. Pasta is a good base for most things but the 'most' was not an option for me. Portuguese supermarkets do a very extensive line in tinned squid but not much else in that genre. The better part of a day was spent buying and packing away my stores which included chorizo, bags of waxed baby bel cheese, armfuls of tinned tripe, 120 tins of squid (assorted sauces), and 135 litres of water (enough for 4 months). I could have done better.

Waiting for the weather is a time honoured activity amongst sailors and I played the game in the first week of January. It was not a case of high winds keeping me in the marina but the opposite in the form of a very light breeze from the south. I saw no point in setting off unless I could make rapid progress straight away. Psychologically there was more of a positive statement of intent with a swift departure and I would benefit from being taken away from the security blanket of land more quickly.

Hanging about the marina, shifting kit around *Aluffe*, checking halyards and passing the time with the winter residents was very easy. Comparing the meagreness of *Aluffe* with the bespoke complexity of Mick and Jo's Bruce Roberts 34 was fascinating. They were live-aboards and had adapted their boat to cater for their every need. But I was procrastinating and wondered if I was finding ways of delaying my departure as an anxiety rose from within me.

Not having seen *Aluffe* for 4 months I had lost that familiar feeling around her and of sailing. It was all coming back fast enough but a sense of finality was settling on me at a time when I felt less prepared than ever before. The next leg would not be similar to the last in that there would be no returning home afterwards. I was going further away from all the comforts that were contained there.

The weather changed for the worse as a front passed through and, wandering along the beach one evening, I watched the large waves breaking on the shore with a sound like thunder. Looking out to sea there were endless rows of powerful waves rolling out of the darkness, black clouds overhead. I imagined myself out there, alone, trying to pick a safe route through the waves with the noise of the wind possibly confusing my judgement. It was an alarming prospect and for the first time I doubted the sense in what I was doing.

With moods as changeable as the weather, however, I was ready to leave on 10th January. The wind was still from the south but a little fresher. Furthermore it was forecast to swing round to the north within 24 hours. Mike, the marina officer, had been very helpful all along but I got the impression he didn't think much of my meteorological skills. Invariably I would study the weather charts in his office and offer my opinion. His head would drop and shake sadly. Other times I would form one based on data gleaned from certain websites. Any plans I made supported by that information would normally draw scorn from Mike who appeared not to trust anything other than his own weather eye, informed by a lifetime in the merchant navy. When I eventually put faith in my own conviction I left with his words of warning about the exceptionally large swell in the area. If I had waited for the all clear from Mike I might never have left until gone April, but he wasn't wrong about the swell.

My ability to move about the boat was appalling as I first headed west to cross the shipping lanes early and get clear of the shallow water. I set a full mainsail and the large genoa for what was ostensibly a beam reach but soon realised that the wind was far too fresh for that arrangement. Going forward to change the genoa for something smaller I found it very difficult to hold my position on the foredeck as *Aluffe* rose and fell a in 2 to 3 metre swell. I faired no better reducing the main where I kept losing my footing. Although far from severe, the conditions were not ideal for me under the circumstances. I was, however, thankful that a change in seasickness pills had worked and there was none of the nausea I had suffered leaving Falmouth.

While physically it was initially difficult to settle the feeling of pleasure at sailing again was immediate. It had been a long process of preparation and talking about the trip, and to be heading out to sea at long last was a relief. As Portugal receded I concentrated on the task of sailing the boat. With all the stores stowed away *Aluffe* had effectively taken on the weight of 3 additional crew. This was in addition to the rest of the heavy kit like the liferaft, deflated tender and fuel. Being small, little things make big differences on *Aluffe* and that extra weight pushed her lower in the water. She was noticeably sluggish and when the wind dropped off she became quite lethargic in responding to the helm. It was a new motion for *Aluffe*, one that I would become used to, but I was grateful that she still managed to cruise at around 4 to 5 knots as we crossed the first set of shipping lanes heading north. As night had fallen I got my head down for a short 30 minute kip while in 'no man's land' in anticipation of having to cross the southbound lane later. Poking my head up for a quick check after my rest I was shocked to see *Aluffe* sandwiched between 2 ships heading north a mile either side. It was a useful reminder that some of the commercial sea jockeys had a fairly casual, if not inaccurate, view of the rules of the road.

The wind did swing to the north as anticipated and remained healthy in the main. Its effect combined with that of the Portugal Current flowing south and *Aluffe* made swift progress. In the first 24 hours she covered 100 miles and in the next 124. I was not shy about using the engine when the wind tailed off as I still wanted to make it to the Canaries without unnecessary delay. I was not aware of being impatient but that distant focus and my gradual adaptation back into life at sea provided a timely reminder of the need for caution.

On day 3 my course took me over a series of sea mounts which rise from the sea bed abruptly and greatly reduce the depth of water in that area. Such lumps under the sea can affect the nature of the waves, making them more agitated. Approaching one I spotted a strange flashing light in the near distance. I couldn't work out what the signal meant but thought it might be someone in trouble. I dropped the foresail and altered course, heading down wind to investigate. At the same time, in anticipation of the need to manoeuvre near the light I released the rope acting to prevent the boom from gybing. Standing up, I steered the boat with the tiller between my legs so my hands were free to prepare lines in the cockpit. Perhaps it was bound to happen, distracted as I was in a lumpy sea, but I lost track of my course and drove too deep, allowing the wind to catch *Aluffe* from a different angle at the stern. The wind filled the wrong side of the mainsail and whipped the boom across the boat very suddenly in a gybe. I sensed the danger and instinctively ducked but was not quick enough. The boom caught me square on the side of the head with a sharp crack, at which point everything slowed down.

There was no pain and I did not lose consciousness but in the moments after the impact my vision was reduced to lots of little green spots flickering on a black background. 'Stay calm!' and 'Think!' were the immediate commands that I forced through my fuzzy mind. I sat in the cockpit and steered the boat a little more to the wind to avoid gybing again. With *Aluffe* settled on a course I was relieved as my sight came back quickly. I looked around me to check that I could focus and that my balance was not suffering. Tentatively I felt around the impact area. Warm and sticky blood seeped from a prominent gash in my throbbing head, soaking my hair and fleece hat.

"Stay calm and think," I repeated out loud.

Very conscious of the fact that I was alone I needed to be very precise in my thinking. Despite the obvious wound and blood my faculties did not seem impaired, and I set the Navic to maintain a safe course. Going below I pulled out the First Aid bag and a mirror for a closer inspection. It didn't look pretty but I did a reasonable job of cleaning and wrapping it up in a dressing. I felt shaken, not so much by the injury but at having made the stupid mistake in the first place. It was a wake up call that my sailing was rusty and a feeling of vulnerability, influenced by the solitude, rested on me. The flashing light had long gone, a fishing boat probably, and so I concentrated on making myself comfortable, drinking water, and getting some rest. Unfortunately I was to get little of the latter that night as *Aluffe* crossed the Ampere Sea Mount in rising and falling winds.

Rather than being able to gather my thoughts and catch up on some sleep *Aluffe* kept me busy as she was pushed about by the disturbed wave patterns. With the wind rising as well I feared that the Navic would not be able to prevent another accidental gybe. I reduced sail and trailed warps from the stern. This had the dual effect of slowing the boat and providing some stability at the stern. It helped the Navic and provided some calm for me while the wind went through its paces. Needless to say the wind dropped off soon after all my efforts to accommodate it but by that time I was more interested in my performance than that of the boat.

I left *Aluffe* as she was and slept below. Lying on my bed I felt pleased at how the night had turned out. No-one likes to get a clout on the head, for obvious reasons, but in the event of it happening, sorting the problem out was, I admitted, the type of trial I had been seeking.

The following day I spoke with Jacqui and my parents but didn't mention the incident of the night before. I did not want to alarm them and could not see the point in telling them then. It was good for me, however, to touch base and useful to get a weather forecast from Dad. He predicted light and variable winds from the south before easterlies would arrive 3 days later. I saw that as a good chance to take things easy for a while but I was not disappointed when the following days were characterised by winds of Force 4 to 6 from the east. I still wanted to get to the Canaries quickly.

Sailing on a beam reach *Aluffe* made very good progress, covering more that 100 miles each day. With blue skies overhead I settled more and more into a rhythm but I could not shake a trace of doubt that was occupying my thoughts. I was surprised by the size of the waves that *Aluffe* was crossing. At nearly 3 metres they were neither large nor insignificant but, while she had their measure, *Aluffe* was getting smacked hard fairly regularly. Thumping into the ones that stood up at just the wrong moment she would shudder and roll with the force. Plumes of spray would regularly break over the side but sometimes a wave would dump its peak on *Aluffe*, on one occasion filling the cockpit. It was all new to me.

The continuous, hard and wearing motion tested both me and *Aluffe*. In those conditions I was aware of how little I could be sure of her strength and capabilities. Amongst the incessant noise of water sluicing past the hull I noticed various creaks and groans, becoming more alarmed when they developed into knocks and bangs. Watching minor bulkheads shifting with the movement of the boat did nothing to sooth my mind and I slept badly. The main hatch caused trouble every time a wave broke over the boat driving water under the runners and dumping it in the cabin and over my bunk. Likewise, the forepeak hatch did not seal properly. In the face of these little things and the remorseless pounding I was becoming more stressed. In response to the gnawing anxiety an old childhood fear of the dark resurfaced and as each night progressed I longed for the dawn of the next day. I began to question whether either I or *Aluffe* was really up for the task. After all my efforts and hopes this was something of a disappointment.

A week after leaving Nazare I arrived in Puerto de San Sebastian on Isla de la Gomera having covered 800 miles. Considering my downbeat mood earlier in the crossing, I was feeling pretty upbeat and had been for a little while. What had been the cause of much of my stress, the non-stop pounding of the boat through the sea, turned out to be the catalyst for a reversal in my spirits. The simple fact was that I could not stop it and, while it was tiring, I got attuned to it. I could not walk away for a break but had to concentrate on eating, navigating, and managing the boat. In the course of doing those the disquiet created by the uncomfortable motion slipped from my attention. Instead I warmed to the sunnier climate, watching female dolphins teaching their calves how to ride the bow and catch waves.

The island of Tenerife appeared late through the mist and I congratulated myself on another successful voyage. Times were not always easy but they were invaluable for the lessons they gave, and *Aluffe* and I were the stronger for them. I never hoped for more and, walking unsteadily along the marina pontoon, I nodded appreciatively at a plan coming together.

The striking beauty of many isolated island groups in the oceans is the result of the volcanic action that created them. La Gomera, in the western part of the Canary Islands, is a good example of this with its dramatic gorges and tall, steep sided valleys. From a distance it is easy to imagine lava flows of old streaming down the slopes, shaping the island into what is now a fertile home for a welcoming local population and a haven for grateful tourists. It does not take long sitting on a boat to lose leg strength. I was determined to build some of mine back up and, after a couple of days getting my bearings, I struck out into the inviting hills adjacent to the marina.

It wasn't the same as conquering a virginal North Face of the Eiger but, in the absence of a trail map that I or any of the local residents I asked could read, being without doubt the first to forge up the scrubby ridge leading away from the marina would do for me. That I was blazing a new trail was writ large on the faces of various farmers and goats-men I met along the way. Appearing from behind obscure rock outcrops and cacti they would give me quizzical looks before waving or nodding cautiously. Happy in my exercise I continued upwards until my state of exhaustion coincided neatly with lunchtime and a minor summit. Far below me was the marina and, chewing on a cheese and pate sandwich, I considered how best to get back.

Referring to the map was of no use because it bore no obvious resemblance to my whereabouts but there appeared to be 2 options available; the road, which twisted its long way down the valley side, or the dry river bed, which twisted almost as much but at the bottom of the valley. I chose the latter and spent the remainder of the afternoon blazing another new route, scrambling over boulders and climbing down waterfalls. Despite the heat it was just what I needed to inject a much needed boost of energy, energy that I could use to tackle the improvements on *Aluffe*.

Top of my hit-list was the disturbing movement of the hatchway bulkhead and the associated banging every time we hit a wave. I fretted about this for a while before clearing everything from the lockers, and contorted myself to a point where I could just grip a through-bolt in the locker while tightening the loose nut the other side of the bulkhead. Every movement inside *Aluffe* had to be well planned for there was precious little space for me to work and I was pleased when all the interior adjustments were completed.

With those out of the way I concentrated on how to keep the water out. I had noticed water seeping in through the port shroud plate. As one of the secure points to which the rigging is attached it needed seeing to. Filling the bolt holes with epoxy-resin before letting them dry and then re-drilling them I improved the fit of the plates. I hoped it would be a good permanent fix.

Moving on to other wet areas I re-lined the forepeak hatch with thick sealing tape but pondered over the main sliding hatch for some time, almost getting to the point of ripping it off altogether and constructing a solid structure in its place. Fortunately, Kai, a helpful passing German boat builder, pointed out the very simple solution of placing a strip of varnished plywood parallel to each of the hatch runners. Whilst not actually making the hatch watertight they would have the effect of dispersing any water rushing along the deck. As a solution for what would be a down wind leg to the Caribbean it worked for me.

Some unseasonal low pressure systems prevented any swift departure which suited me fine while I got myself together and attended to *Aluffe*. There were plenty of distractions in the marina, in particular the presence of 2 solo Atlantic rowers. Bhavik was intending to become the first Asian to row the Atlantic in his modern boat which was as long as *Aluffe*. The other rower was Graham Walters, 59 years old and from Leicester. He was an old hand at the game having crossed 3 times previously. For his fourth attempt he had pressed into service the infamous *Puffin* which had lost its original 2 man crew in 1966. *Puffin* was recovered after a storm and placed in a museum but the 2 men hoping to set a record for the fastest crossing of the Atlantic west to east were never found. Graham was at least hoping to complete the task of getting *Puffin* across the Atlantic albeit using a different route. Both he and Bhavik, however, had been caught up in some dubious Spanish bureaucracy and been forced to delay their original departure date. Most of the trouble surrounding safety gear and government permissions had been resolved with the payment of large bonds and they hoped to be leaving soon.

Speaking to the earthy Graham I was struck by his extraordinary self effacing nature which seemed at odds for someone with the experience he had gathered and the ambition he displayed. He just got on with what he had to do without any fuss and if he hadn't kept returning to this awkward looking tub I would have never have guessed what he was up to. My assertions about *Puffin* were correct and she did not row any better than she looked. Weighing in at 2.5 tonnes and measuring 16 foot in length she was awful to row when I tried. Graham best described rowing *Puffin* as like 'dragging piles of bricks through wet cement'. He was a very determined man beneath the amiable surface and I wished him every success.

Bhavik was very different to Graham. He was one of the first people I met when I landed in San Sebastian and very approachable. He pointed out the main points of interest around the marina when I arrived and bought me a beer for brunch. He was definitely very determined to complete his challenge having had to jump through so many hoops and invest so much to get to the start line.

Jacqui and I sailing *Aluffe* pre-refit off Pendennis Castle, Falmouth, UK

Aluffe in January 2007 prior to launching in Nazare, Portugal. A 32ft Vancouver on the left provides a sense of scale.

Provisioning in Portugal with 5 months of tinned squid.
I could have done better.

Seeking inspiration from RKJ on passage to Barbados.

A large colony of gooseneck barnacles took up residence on *Aluffe's* hull crossing from the Canaries.

Footpath to Victoria Falls, Dominica.

Hard at work on *Tiziana*, Antigua Classic Week.

Gli-Gli and her Carib Indian crew on tour through the Caribbean.

Graham Walters and *Puffin* off St Barts
100 days after leaving La Gomera, Canaries.

For the tenacity and commitment he had already shown he deserved ultimate success. And yet there was nothing in the manner of his preparation during the week and a half I was there that suggested he would be. He did virtually nothing to repair the obvious faults on his boat, relying instead on others, myself included, to do the lion's share of getting them sorted. His practical aptitude was no better than his athleticism. He was a big chap but hardly toned and honed for the job. I had it on good authority that he couldn't row, either. Rather than practise he was often seen sipping wine and beer in the bars in the middle of the day, moving on to the clubs at night. By the time I left I was genuinely concerned for him and asked him if he really knew what he was taking on. He gave me the same answer that I gave to everyone who asked me the same question.

"Not really, but that's why I am trying. I want to find out what it is like and how I will react. I'll find out when it happens. I can't do it any other way."

Suitably chastened I wished him well.

"And you, William. Have a good trip yourself. Maybe I'll see you in Antigua."

There was a chance that our paths could cross in Antigua. If they did I would gladly buy him a drink.

Before I left I wanted to walk in the Parque Nacional de Garajonay. Situated in the middle of the island it stretches over 3,948 hectares and has been designated a World Heritage Site. A cloud of mist covers the area for much of the year and the park consequently possesses a lush forest containing a wide variety of trees. It is the only survivor of the forests that grew along the shores of the Mediterranean before disappearing after the Ice Ages. To get the best view of it I climbed Alto de Garajonay, the park's highest peak at 1,487 metres and then descended through the forest. Standing at the top, despite the mist, Tenerife, La Gomera's neighbouring island to the east, was clearly visible. Facing to the south-west I saw a sailing boat heading south, presumably to the Cape Verde Islands or the Caribbean. The boat was a minute white pin prick on a vast expanse of blue sea. And yet for the crew it was their world and would be their home for the next few weeks. I imagined their mixed moods and anticipated mine.

I dropped from the summit into the cool forest. The freshness of the mist and mountain air was no cleaner than the sea air, but the salt always adds a touch of harshness to the vigour it provides. I have often debated where the best place to live would be – in the mountains or by the sea. Invariably I have sat on the fence but in La Gomera the argument was solved by having the best of both worlds.

I made my way down to the village of Hermigua in the east of the park. It was my intention to walk all the way back to San Sebastian but, confronted by a monster climb out of the village and the prospect of a 12 kilometre walk after that, I took refuge in the Bar Los Amigos and waited for a bus. It was a quiet bar with only a few locals. I drank my beer, occasionally joining the banter in faltering Spanish, but the cosy ambience altered with the arrival of the village idiot. Everyone else recognised him immediately and melted away as he threw himself through the door laughing loudly at the cracks in the floor. Becoming the obvious target for his attentions I spent the next hour talking complete rubbish with him during which time the clearest statement he managed to make was 'Estas loco! Estas loco!' ('You are crazy! You are crazy!')

'Hello,' I thought, 'who have you been talking to?'

By 29th January, after 11 days in San Sebastian, the weather, *Aluffe*, and I were all fully primed for an exit into the Atlantic. I had been informed by an ex-navy man that there was no virtue in being adamant about destinations in case plans changed or the navigation messed up. I subsequently took to telling everyone that I was heading towards Barbados rather than actually going to the distant island.

I would be leaving in the company of *Dart Warrior*, a Warrior 35, and her crew, skippered by a dreadlocked Kieran. In search of love and land he was on an extended trip around the world. He almost achieved it in the Mediterranean but had moved on taking on board 2 diving instructors, Maxine and Fontaine, for the ocean crossing. Kieran was a wind surfer and did not travel without his kit strapped around the aft cabin. Fontaine added his surf board to the pile, while his diving gear and that of Maxine was stored in the aft cabin with them. At rest *Dart Warrior* had a serious lifting of the bows with all the weight collected at the stern. Performance wise it made no sense but in the event it worked well. With the draw of the sails pulling the boat forward the stern naturally lifted and the boat ran flat through the water.

Kieran, Maxine and Fontaine were a generous crowd and it was good to be leaving in their company. The idea of sharing the moment with another boat rested well with me without any crew of my own to recognise the occasion. We would no doubt get separated within a few hours as they would be taking a route fractionally to the south heading towards the Cape Verde islands. They were planning a short stop there before continuing towards Barbados where I hoped we might meet up again and swap tales of high adventure.

At last, at 1400 hours, after a round of goodbyes with the other yachties in the marina and to the rowers, we shoved off in sunshine with a brisk 15 to 20 knots of wind chasing us out of the harbour. *Aluffe* was carrying 2 reefs in the main and a baby jib. Bubbling with excitement I jumped about and ‘yahoo-ed’ loudly at the onset of my first ocean crossing.

Chapter 6
First ocean crossing

Aluffe and *Dart Warrior* used the best of the fresh breeze to pace each other south-west from La Gomera. The island has been a traditional stepping off point for many Atlantic crossings since Christopher Columbus did so in 1492 in search of the New World. To know the thoughts of the sailors on board the *Santa Maria, Pinta*, and *Santa Clara*, setting out for the first time into the unknown would be priceless, and I wondered how they compared with mine. I could only hope that we shared to at least a small degree the same mix of thrill and tension that comes at the beginning of a voyage.

From all the books, films and stories that abound today about the Atlantic I had the benefit of knowing what could be expected. Being clear about to where it was I was heading and how far away it lay was a big advantage over my medieval counterparts. There was greater certainty in my mind that the warm trade winds and the North Equatorial Current would be travelling with me towards the Caribbean. Rather than fear being set upon by freak waves breaking dangerously over the boat, as those ancient sailors might, I could anticipate being waved along by the now renowned Atlantic rollers, building steadily over the 2500 mile journey. Also, despite some high profile accounts of whales sinking boats, I could be fairly confident I would not be attacked by an enormous sea monster from the deep.

There were no guarantees that those balmy conditions would remain constant throughout, however, raising a note of caution. The fact that the world's weather has become more changeable and unpredictable through climate change was enough to allay any false sense of security. I had come to believe that the unexpected might happen, as opposed to just could. That, and the fact that I would be confronting everything on my own and for the first time, left me feeling edgy despite the overwhelming euphoria at heading towards the first golden sunset of the crossing.

After plenty of shouting and waving the 2 boats drifted apart as *Dart Warrior* turned a little further to the south and *Aluffe* dropped back with a dying wind. Having decided not to use the engine on the crossing unless the solar panel failed to keep the batteries charged, I could only watch as Kieran and friends motored over the horizon on passage to the Cape Verde Islands. I carried enough fuel on board for 150 miles at the most. Over the distance of the leg it would be pointless to think motoring in any calmer patches would make any worthwhile difference. Nonetheless, it would have been encouraging to think that before sunset I could have left La Gomera well behind. Instead, I struggled with a fickle wind and a mounting frustration. Unfortunately, my fracturing mood took another knock with the demise of the very useful but ancient auto-tiller.

Attached to the tiller when we motored or sailed in light winds, the auto-tiller ran off the batteries and maintained the perfect compass course. The oddly grating sound it made with its small, sharp adjustments had become quite companionable. Sadly, it chose the first few hours of the leg to start stuttering before giving up the ghost completely. Poking around in its innards did nothing to bring it back to life, and I was forced to accept I would have only the Navic to back me up. This was far from a crisis in light of my vow of abstinence but its passing removed a thin layer of security of which I had not previously been aware.

To sail solo over a distance without some form of self steering is an old skill, but no small undertaking either. It is possible to balance most boats in some conditions by lashing the tiller in a central position and adjusting the sails to suit. Robin Knox-Johnston successfully demonstrated this when he sailed his boat, *Suhaili*, half way around the world in 1969 after his self steering gear failed. Alternatively, there are various 'sheet to tiller' arrangements, whereby the sheet of the foresail is attached to the tiller. This in turn is held along the centre line by bungee chord, providing an equal but opposing force. If the boat is well balanced in the first place it will maintain its course as the sails fill and spill with the rise and fall of the wind. These and other systems can be effective but do not compare with specific self steering gear, like *Aluffe's* Navic. I would not have contemplated leaving without one. Unfortunately, the Navic, whilst pin-point accurate upwind, was less capable in light airs and downwind, as the apparent wind flowing over the vane was reduced.

The Navic struggled with the conditions off La Gomera on that first evening while I fixed myself a much needed meal. We were a few miles from the shores of the island but close enough to be caught in its wind shadow. The whispers of wind eddied around us throwing the Navic into confusion. Trying to ignore the wayward course *Aluffe* was being taken on I cooked up a large pan of pasta and squid with vegetables to bolster my spirits. Annoyingly, I lost my grip on the pan handle and managed only to spill its contents over the cockpit before a mouthful was taken. Picking the cooling, oily food off the deck I sincerely hoped that this inauspicious start was not to be the way of things to come.

If it had been my wish to be out of sight of land by the morning after a fitful sleep I was to be disappointed by the continued presence of the island of Hierro which remained irritatingly on show for most of the next day. An otherwise tedious day combating the light northerly winds was lifted for a while by the raising of the spinnaker, which I had insisted on carrying with me. I had flown it for the first time on passage to Nazare and discovered then that I had to be very choosy over the conditions. It was foolish to try flying it in winds above a Force 4 or in a choppy sea. *Aluffe* would start to sway and the large sail would become potentially difficult to handle if the weather worsened. If the wind was too light the sail collapsed whenever a wave tipped the boat one way or the other. With a flat sea and steady gentle breeze, however, the spinnaker was a must.

The act of getting the voluminous sail into the air was not difficult once the spinnaker pole was set and the lines were locked off in roughly the right places to provide it with immediate shape after it was raised. Sailing downwind I would quickly haul it out of the bag on the halyard and up the mast. Adjusting the control lines, the sheet and guy, the bright yellow, red and black spinnaker would balloon out and draw *Aluffe* forward with extra pace and purpose. It was not a case of sitting back and letting *Aluffe* and the Navic get on with it, however, as the latter was hopeless at driving with the spinnaker up, easily becoming disorientated. It was necessary for me to drive while playing the sheet one handed to best effect. If I tired I would lock the sheet off, steering a course that suited the sail or it would collapse loudly, shaking the rig.

Getting the spinnaker down again only took a few seconds. Standing in the cockpit, I would de-power the sail by releasing the sheet and guy, and then drag it straight into the cabin, steering all the while with the tiller between my knees. It was to avoid any snarl ups in that precarious position that the kite only flew on a relatively flat sea. The appearances of the spinnaker were subsequently rare, but each time was a morale booster, fully justifying the expense.

The first week out proved, however, those colourful bonus moments aside, that not far beneath the positive and confident mood that had shown itself on La Gomera, lay evidence of a more serious and distressing sense of vulnerability. The frustration I had felt on the first night, the occasional bout of nausea, and a darkening frame of mind were all signs that I was struggling to settle into the passage. The all consuming effort required to sail the boat that had been so liberating heading to Portugal took me as an unwilling hostage leaving the Canaries.

As the winds picked up, so did the pace of *Aluffe* with an accompanying increase in noise and movement. I was used to the behaviour of *Aluffe* by then and the difficulty there was in finding a stable and comfortable position in the cramped cabin. Leaving the Navic to drive, I would sit at the top end of my berth on the starboard side, leaning against the galley. Putting my left foot against the steps leading into the cabin and my right against the liferaft on the port berth, I jammed myself into a position that allowed me to eat, write and doze. But for the first time I found the idea of sticking it out for over 3 weeks intimidating. I imagined being back at home working a full 5 day week, and following it up with a busy weekend cycling, walking the dog and meeting up with friends. There seemed to be an incredible amount that could be fitted into 7 days and I saw it as a long and productive period. Looking around me, facing the unfamiliar on my own, and 7 days became an almost unbearable sentence. The prospect was not improved when I dwelt on the fact that such a period would have to be repeated at least 3 times in succession. Nearly a month or one twelfth of a year, would pass before I next saw land or spoke to someone face to face.

Whereas I had once looked forward to experiencing such solitude, my mood then sank at what had become a depressing notion. I became languid and stared for long hours into the distance, my mind churning over the distressing thought that I had jumped into something far beyond my limits. I had tackled the voyage with the same enthusiasm and belief that had seen me through Ironman competitions, and a 6 day 900 mile cycle-ride from Lands End to John O'Groats. There were low moments on each of those, and other events, but I always recovered and completed them. And yet, it seemed different without the option to draw breath and escape from the hectic pace being set by *Aluffe*. After a slow start our progress was rapid and by the end of the first week we recorded a high average of 110 miles a day. For much of it I just wanted everything to stop as my resolve showed signs of crumbling completely.

I could not see a way out at first, but instead considered all the scenarios that would see me returning home without the boat. I thought of finding a ship on which to transport *Aluffe* back, or selling her, when I reached the Caribbean. Both options would be costly but I couldn't care less. The thought of scuttling the boat and setting off the EPIRB, my emergency satellite beacon, was one ridiculous option for a time while I became ensnared in a state of despair. All the incredulity and misgivings expressed by so many people in the UK and since then began to haunt me as my self-assurance was undermined by a fear of impending failure. How many wry grins did I see on the faces of my doubters in that first week? How many 'Told you so's' did I hear uttered from their lips?

I tried desperately to shake myself back onto an even keel. I rationalised with myself, breaking the trip down into days, and the days into hours, setting myself small targets to achieve. It was easy to see what was going wrong, and likewise, how to start the process of building myself back up again, but I slipped too easily from bouts of melancholy to periods of exuberance. In my isolation I became increasingly sensitive, and my reactions to the ever changing thoughts rattling around my head were often exaggerated as a consequence. If I thought of something funny I would laugh out aloud, and similarly tears would flow if I dwelt on a sad memory.

Going up on deck on Day 4 I was more amused than alarmed by the huge cargo ship, *Lady Copacabana*, which suddenly appeared and powered past 200 metres to starboard. It did not bother me that I was obviously entirely unsighted by the crew, indicating how I still retained a robust streak. Despite that evidence of some acceptance of my circumstances, however, I would invariably slip back under the undeniable truth that *Aluffe* was still surrounded by endless sea, she was still yawing uncomfortably, and I was still lonely.

It was not just I who suffered in the mire of my dejected mind, which extended its dark tentacles beyond the realms of my immediate rocking world. Kieran, Maxine, Fontaine, Graham, and Bhavik, along with the Atkins, a Canadian family on another yacht, *Medley*, which left La Gomera on the same day as I, all perished at sea. They were absurd and nonsensical thoughts and I told myself as much, but tears still welled up in my eyes. Furthermore, I felt ashamed at having the audacity to question the intentions of Bhavik when I so blatantly didn't have the faintest idea what I was talking about.

As we headed further towards more southerly latitudes the winds became more consistent from the north-east despite a few hours of lighter wind most nights. We were still covering good ground each day, including a 136 mile run on the fifth day, but this was pushing *Aluffe* too much for my nerves. On 3 occasions she had gybed as a result of carrying too much sail in waves of up to 3 metres. I was all for covering the distance as quickly as possible, mainly to reduce the amount of time I would have to spend on my own, but also in deference to my competitive nature. However, the need to look after myself on a passage of this length was obvious to see in the more lucid moments.

There was no incentive, no race or reward, for a fast crossing and so there was no reason to raise the level of risk to either me or *Aluffe*. There had to be a way of eradicating the tendency, albeit a rare one, of the boat to gybe accidentally. It was not the incident itself that caused me concern which was quite a gentle sequence of events. *Aluffe* would rotate around her keel, point too low downwind allowing the breeze to back the main and then slowly shift over onto her new leeward side. There was rarely any drama as I had a boom preventer permanently attached after my experience heading to the Canaries. Having gybed I would release the main, get her back up to speed for control and then gybe her back. The stress I felt was the anticipation of it happening, preventing me from resting properly.

Part of the cause of the involuntary gybes was the excessive drive produced by the mainsail prompting *Aluffe* to try and round up into the wind. Countering this effect was the pressure in the foresail, which was invariably poled out to windward with the wind coming from behind as the boat sailed on a very broad reach. With too much sail up *Aluffe* would be under extra pressure and zigzag wildly as the Navic worked harder to maintain the boat's course. The Navic had to cope not only with powerful sails, but also with waves that were perfectly capable of grabbing *Aluffe*'s stern and dragging it to either side. If the wind was strong enough the Navic could more often than not direct *Aluffe* back on course. If, however, the waves were the controlling force, the Navic would be slow to respond and *Aluffe* could gybe.

Despite carrying 6 foresails I was not in a position to fly 2 at the same time, efficiently balanced with the mainsail packed away. This would have offered the benefit of drawing the boat forward from the bows and negating the chances of turning into the wind. The Navic would have been far more effective with that set-up but had to settle with a readiness on my part to reduce sail, particularly the mainsail, early and at night. By underplaying the mainsail, *Aluffe* was not under so much pressure from the rig. She swayed less and the Navic managed a more positive course. Whilst a fraction of speed had been lost, the Navic steered a less frantic course and, most importantly, I could relax more easily.

The seriousness of my position made me look at the satellite phone I was carrying in a different light. Originally I had accepted it for emergencies and weather information only. It was never my intention to spend hours nattering randomly to names in my address book, and getting weather reports from my dad was only ever going to be a brief exchange on an occasional basis. I had always wanted the intensity of being 'out there', pushing boundaries on my own without assistance, all of which I believed would make for a greater achievement. It is arguable, however, that because it was on board, acting as a point of temptation, the phone added to my distress, making me more aware of how lonely I felt. Be that as it may, I fully appreciated by that stage how very real my circumstances were and how difficult I was finding them. The idea that I should add to my problems by refusing myself the option of talking to friends and family seemed plain silly. The trip was developing into something that was plenty big enough for me. Depriving myself of the use of the telephone for a proper chat was a contrived and unnecessary hardship. Simply by accepting that it was ok to use the phone if I wanted to reduced the weight I had placed on my shoulders immediately. Speaking with Jacqui, my parents and friends after that was still rare and problematic because reception was all too often poor, but sharing the experience was more rewarding than I had previously imagined it might be.

Boredom was a major cause of my troubles, and one I had always known I would have to confront. My intention had been to listen to music on the Single-Side-Band radio I carried on board but it rarely picked up any clear signal leaving me to rely on a harmonica that I thought I might learn along the way. Unfortunately, without a book to teach me it was not the best comfort or distraction.

Fortunately, a variety of books had made it aboard to help me while away the hours and my recovery continued as I read '*A World of My Own*', Robin Knox-Johnston's account of his epic, and the first ever, solo non-stop circumnavigation of the world. I became enthralled by this remarkable man who conquered a peak long thought impossible. His level of seamanship and that of mine were worlds apart, as was his matter of fact attitude to getting on with the job. As *Suhaili* suffered knock downs and breakages, her sails falling apart around him, Knox-Johnston went about fixing them, daubing Stockholm Tar on fittings and carrying out regular maintenance with a degree of resourcefulness that was inspiring. If I had thought Stockholm Tar might help my situation and I knew what it was I would have gladly splashed the stuff liberally on all parts of *Aluffe*.

In the main a small, glass-fibre sailboat does not require much regular maintenance but lying awake with my thoughts on the sixth night I listened to the creaking and banging from the hatchway bulkhead that had returned. It was one o'clock in the morning and I was tired and stressed. The banging noise signified that *Aluffe* was shaking herself loose in the Atlantic conditions. I felt annoyed for remaining in my prone position, hoping pathetically that it would stop. I had a pretty good idea what RKJ would do if he were me. It was a reproachful thought and it tipped me over the edge.

"Right. Bugger this, William. Get a grip!" I commanded loudly.

Ignoring the difficulties posed by the darkness and the gyrations of the boat, I cleared the port berth of the boxes lying on it, along with the liferaft. Opening up the lockers either side of the bulkhead I cleared them of squid, water bottles, vegetables, nuts and tinned fruit, stacking them untidily in the forepeak with the sails. Armed with the necessary tools I twisted my body into the required knot and made a fix that would last for the remainder of the crossing. When everything was re-stowed in their original places I continued my good work, greasing the prop flange, and fiddling with the electrics before lying back satisfied on the mattress. Taking the more positive and proactive approach to solving my troubles was clearly the way to go and there was no merit in getting wound up about things I could no longer control, like solitude, and the welfare of my fellow sailors.

We maintained a south-south-west course for the first week with the intention of picking up the predictable easterly trade winds before bearing west across the Atlantic. It took us within a few hundred miles of the Cape Verde Islands and a deviation was a tempting option although never seriously entertained. To put an end to my rollercoaster ride or at least break the journey had merit in theory but realistically I never felt I couldn't eventually get myself together. And so it proved to be the case as the efforts to raise my spirits began to pay off and I continued towards Barbados with a growing interest and confidence.

Having worked out a better way to control both the boat and my spirits a more settled composure returned, and I took far more interest and pleasure in all around me. There had been very little in the way of visible marine life along the way apart from the odd collection of dolphins joining me for brief moments and the regular visitations from the seabirds. Approaching the mid-way point I met my first tropicbird. They are striking birds and look out of place at sea with their 2 long tail feathers trailing behind their white bodies. Unlike shearwaters the tropicbird didn't seem comfortable relying on the updraft that could be gained from gliding close to the water's surface. Instead it approached *Aluffe* at masthead height beating its wings anxiously, complementing the look on its face. It cocked its head towards me as if searching for a place to perch and rest up. After a few twitchy passes it obviously thought better of attempting a landing on such a precarious platform and set off. I last saw it heading in the direction of the Cape Verde Islands, nearly 700 miles upwind. It made flying look like hard work and I couldn't help but think it had made a bad choice.

Progressing steadily across the Atlantic *Aluffe* began to disturb more and more flying fish in the warmer waters. Cutting through the water her bow would spark off sudden explosions of activity as the fish tried to avoid the new predator. With urgent flicks of their tails they would launch themselves into the air and spread their translucent wings. Catching the wind they would glide great distances. I estimated the longest flight to last nearly 20 seconds and covered a distance of over 200 metres. Sometimes a flight would be near its end before a well timed flick of the tail on a wave extended it for a little while longer.

It was an impressive display of a unique defensive ploy against their main predator, the tuna. Unfortunately for the flying fish the tuna are very fast swimmers with, apparently, good eyesight. Having watched their prey take to the air tuna don't just give up but follow the fish in flight from below the surface. Swimming as fast as the fish can fly the tuna are well placed when their meal lands with a splash in their wide open jaws. Nonetheless, it remains a fascinating example of nature's ability to adapt, and I often considered in which direction along that evolutionary path were the flying fish travelling.

A friend of mine in Cornwall, Jez, no stranger to adventure and barren places himself having spent 2 years mountaineering in the Antarctic, had given me a present before I left. On the wrapping he had written: 'To be opened at 39 degrees west'. That point of longitude was roughly the mid way point between La Gomera and Barbados, and I reached it on 11th February, Day 14, having covered 1500 miles. I am not a regular drinker but am far from being abstemious. It was my preference, however, not to carry any drink on board, preferring to run a dry boat for my trip in order to keep my wits about me. Given my dire state of mind in the previous days that was probably no bad thing. It is depressing enough to drink alone, and starting depressed cannot make the occasion any more light hearted. The sharp taste of Glenfiddich that Jez had generously provided for me in a classy pewter flask, however, was like nectar.

Speaking to him that night I appreciated the opportunity to jabber away about the highs and lows with someone who could at least partially empathise with my situation. He claimed no surprise at how I was feeling and was impressed by what I was doing. I reflected on that later and it did strike me that I had come a long way and was far better equipped for all my experiences to continue further still.

Sailing the boat was technically not difficult. The wind never blew from in front of *Aluffe*'s stern quarters the whole way across and only on rare occasions did it increase in strength to beyond 25 knots, or Force 6. I regularly took the helm to keep my hand in and to make best use of the waves when they increased with a building wind. The big difference between self-steering gear and humans, beyond the obvious, is that humans are proactive whilst the former can only be reactive. The ability for a person to anticipate the effect of an approaching wave or gust allows him or her to purposefully choose a course, be it to catch a wave for a boost in performance or to take avoiding action. This does not mean that *Aluffe* would not surf without me on the helm – she reached over 15 knots while I slept once – but it is very much down to chance. If it were not, however, for the drama provided by irregular squalls the sailing content of the crossing would have been quite dull.

Spotting the path and imminent arrival of a squall was easy. A feature of the crossing was the blue sky above dotted with white puffy clouds. Each one denoted a spot of extra wind beneath it to push the boat along just that little bit more for a few minutes. An approaching grey cloud, often with a veil of rain hanging beneath it, in amongst the puffy collection indicated a squall. The darker the cloud, the more intense the change in wind speed and the fall of rain. I welcomed those squalls as an antidote to the increasing heat and bright sunshine. They provided bursts of exhilarating speed and the opportunity for a wash.

I had catered for 3 litres of water each day to cover all my drinking, cooking and washing needs. In reality I was using less than 2, partly because I drank too little and washed the dishes in seawater, but also because I rarely washed thoroughly. For the purposes of hygiene I brushed my teeth and used wet wipes in the appropriate places, but travelling alone and with a poor sense of smell, I did not often feel the need to wash my hair, shave or scrub myself down all over regularly. The process of successfully pulling off any of them required high levels of balance, patience and dexterity, the 3 of which coincided all too infrequently. The arrival of a more sustained squall or a band of low pressure, however, called for a removal of any clothing and a cracking open of the shower gel.

The normal sequence of events started with a swift increase in wind and some building up of the waves. After a few minutes, sometimes longer, the rain would be dumped from on high. White out conditions would fill in as a barrage of water from above reduced the waves in an instant to mere fractions of their former glory. The wind also dropped slightly and so, if the Navic had not been entrusted with driving, I would steer with either one leg or with the tiller between my knees depending if I was able to stand or had to sit. Taking a good dollop of gel to rub over me I would make a thick lather before it was washed off by the rain. In the same way that persistent blue-tack might be worked off a wall so I rubbed my skin drawing off the accumulated layers of sweat, sun-cream, dead skin and grime. New and pristine skin surfaced gleaming with vitality like the plants on a parched African plain after the long awaited rains. Revitalised and invigorated I treated myself to a clean t-shirt which I would wear that night to prevent myself from sticking to the mattress and sheet as the nights got muggier heading west.

A squall caught me by surprise one night and I missed the opportunity to scrub up, but it did create its own drama. I lay, as I always did, on a mattress on the cabin floor. It was a tiny space 4.5 feet long and a little over one foot wide, and seemingly not an obvious place to lie. With a mattress from one of the berths underneath it was possible to get comfortable even though I had to draw my legs up making it look as if I was preparing for a gynaecological examination. Most importantly, however, it put me close to the centre of the boat level with the water. Locked into my cramped position I was subjected to no more than a gentle motion no matter what the conditions outside, and I used to sleep quite well, if fitfully. Soundly asleep that night, I was slow to react to the sudden arrival of a nasty squall and woke, alert to *Aluffe* twisting sharply and changing her angle to the wind and waves. The wind had picked up to 30 knots quickly, gybing the boat, and was now pressing her hard as she was carrying too much sail.

Naked, I ducked through the hatch, into the cockpit, and released the boom preventer. The working jib was poled out to leeward as a result of the gybe and flapped furiously. The wind hammered through the rigging and *Aluffe* was tossed about by a large and agitated sea. I jumped up to the mast, released the main halyard and put the third reef in the main. The sheets to the jib whipped violently across the foredeck in the dark but I found myself laughing at the comical scene as I pulled the sail down. It is said that men cannot multi-task but I considered my efforts to stay on board, desperately trying to reduce sail whilst protecting my manhood, as proof to the contrary. Having settled the boat down and fixed the Navic, which had broken a universal joint during the gybe, I lay back on my mattress, content at having dealt calmly with the minor crisis. It had been an instinctive response without any panic and I found that heartening and proof that I was becoming more adept at sea.

The rhythm of my days became fairly standard with the accumulation of miles covered and Barbados drew ever closer. The main meal in the evening had been joined by a more substantial breakfast of cereal and peanut butter on crackers at the other end of the day. I included fruit while it lasted but settled for nuts after the second week. Breakfast would be 'earned' by making a proper assessment of the conditions and the state of the boat soon after day break. Once the cabin was tidy and the galley was packed away I tended to drive for a while before the sun pursued me back into the shade of the cabin. If the boat was on starboard tack, with the mainsail on the port side and to the south, I would find a protected spot on the deck. However, often the most comfortable place to be was back on my mattress on the floor of the cabin and I did spend long hours there reading the likes of Dickens and Alan Bennett, neither of whom I would have otherwise enjoyed. Unfortunately, my small library could not keep up with my appetite for the written word and by the time I reached Barbados I had been reduced to reading the labels on food packaging and one of John Simpson's autobiographies.

Midday would be the occasion for a fix of my position. This was a simple case of taking my position off the GPS (not yet having mastered the sextant), checking the distance covered on the log, and plotting my position on the chart. Making simple notes in the ship's log about our heading with a weather report was all I deemed necessary even though some sailors will update hourly, writing reams of information. The most important aspect of this activity to me, apart from noting where I was, was seeing how far I had travelled in the past 24 hours. It was a small challenge for me to keep *Aluffe* moving as efficiently as I could as the circumstances dictated. With the aid of the current, which gifted us 15 miles each day, we would regularly cover about 120 miles. I got very excited and had a tot of Jez's whisky on Day 19 when we managed a record 138 miles.

In the days that followed, however, I couldn't put my finger on why our mileages appeared to drop off despite good conditions. *Aluffe* just didn't seem to be hitting the average or the surf speeds to which I had become accustomed. A fresh coat of antifouling had been applied in Nazare and the hull was clean before I left La Gomera, and so I could not imagine that I would have collected any significant quantity of weed over 3 weeks. I didn't go for a swim but, leaning as far out as I could, the hull appeared smooth. I had to shrug the mystery off and continue on my way.

To save weight and expense *Aluffe* did not carry a generator or a wind turbine, but I was not keen on running the engine and relied on the solar panel to charge the batteries. Subsequently when it got dark soon after I had eaten I would drop below and sleep for the night. Sometimes I would gaze at the vast array of stars in the sky and marvel at my idiocy at not bringing a star guide. After each hour of sleeping I would automatically wake up and check for any lights. There is every sense in keeping a lookout at all times but on my own it was not feasible. My regular checks were better than nothing although I saw only one light on my last night at sea during the whole crossing. I did wonder how effective my brief looks actually were, when *Aluffe* could have been unsighted in the trough of a wave as might have been another ship nearby. There had to be an element of playing the odds, a game which is not uncommon on boats taking the same route.

Perhaps I should have anticipated it but as we closed to within the last 200 miles of Barbados the wind began to drop off and our daily runs with it. Despite the obvious frustration I was very settled in my routine and had become happy with the idea of continuing. I think this may have been a similar reaction to the one I had after my bungee jump mistake when I claimed to be gagging to have another go. 'Sadly' on that occasion there was a queue and my fellow travellers and I had to leave, by which time I had calmed down and begun to see reason. Likewise, with the hard bit done and the scent of victory in the air I had an emboldened feeling of wishing to continue sailing. I could not deny, however, as I struggled to keep the sails filled and avoid the temptation of putting the engine on, my eyes were peeled and my neck craned as I sought the first sight of land.

Poking my head up at dawn on February 22nd I looked eagerly to the horizon ahead and was momentarily startled by the disappointment I felt at the sight of Barbados sliding rather hesitantly towards me. Unlike the striking volcanic island of La Gomera my Caribbean destination was low lying to a fault and completely misrepresented the sense of achievement I had begun to feel. Nonetheless, the thought of a mid afternoon rum punch galvanised me into action. The wind was a dribbling affair and the swell was coming uncomfortably from the starboard stern quarter making it difficult to hold a sensible amount of sail. With the sweet taste of Barbados's finest Mount Gay rum all but on my lips I finally cracked and turned the engine over. It fired up and I did my customary look over the stern to check the cooling water was flowing correctly. No cooling water. Shutting the engine off again I shook my head at the injustice. A quick search located a degraded impellor in the water pump. With a fresh one installed the engine ran smoothly and I settled back to watch Barbados gradually fill my view.

Rounding Needham Point at the south west corner of the island I turned into Carlisle Bay, the beach front to the capital, Bridgetown. A cocktail of adrenalin and relief swept through me as I gazed at the sweeping sandy beach. It acted as a fine white divide between the palm trees and buildings on the far side, and the yachts bobbing at anchor in the clear water to the fore. Harbour control told me to anchor in Carlisle Bay and check in with them the next day as it was busy. This suited me well. The thought of dealing with customs and paper work at such a high point did not appeal and so, bubbling with elation, I motored closer in to shore for a suitable spot to finally stop.

Passing through the small collection of other yachts at anchor I recognised *Medley*, the 50 footer that had left La Gomera on the same day as I, and started to talk. I blabbered, in fact, as words that couldn't get out fast enough tumbled from my mouth, tripping over each other so eager were they to be heard by another person. Tying up alongside *Medley*, I didn't admit to the Canadians that I had killed them off a few weeks before, but gratefully accepted the offer of a rum punch, gladly drinking to their health instead. Travelling much faster than I they had stopped off in the Cape Verde Islands and arrived in Carlisle Bay the day before. They had been in touch with Kieran, who also appeared to be alive, and thought he would be arriving in the next few days. We chatted for a while, appreciating the magnitude of each others crossing before I made off a little way to anchor.

At 4 o'clock in the afternoon I dropped the pick onto the seabed after 24 days and 2 hours at sea. I had achieved a milestone in seafaring and allowed myself a slap on the back for that. It was my first ocean crossing and solo to boot, which accounted for an odd sense of bewilderment mixed with surprise and relief. Despite the occasional drama the trip had been largely uneventful and not made up of significant highs and lows, despite the trauma of the first week. It had been rather more an ebb and flow of personal contentment and apprehension. Sailing the boat had not posed any insurmountable problems but an undercurrent of anxiety, born of my lack of experience, was ever present. There had been much to learn on a daily basis where common sense, caution and patience had become my greatest allies. 2800 miles is a very long way, but no less was the mental mileage covered. In the first week out *Aluffe* was destined to return on a ship, but there was no doubt upon arriving in Barbados that we would be sailing back together.

I celebrated with Jacqui and called my parents. Speaking with my dad on the satellite phone he was equally jubilant as I jabbered away and thanked him for being on hand for support and the weather. I think he still had some fears about me returning on the trickier west-east route but for the time being we shared the success. As we chatted a green-back turtle surfaced close by to *Aluffe* as if in greeting. It wasn't the graceful mermaid I may have wished for but I accepted the invitation anyway. Stripping off my shorts, I dived into the freshness of the water, swimming deep before erupting at the surface to release all my remaining tension. How the sailors with Columbus must have enjoyed a similar moment in the Caribbean waters over 500 years before.

Chapter 7
Caribbean island hopping

Bridgetown awoke slowly, as did I after a night ashore to celebrate my arrival. Strictly speaking I should have remained on *Aluffe* until clearing customs but the lure of conversation and rum proved too strong. Watching the early morning joggers on the beach from my vantage point of the appreciatively still deck of *Aluffe* I sipped a reviving cup of tea, warming myself in the first rays of the Caribbean sun. Whilst Barbados as an island crept over the horizon almost apologetically, the Bajans themselves are the polar opposite. The solitude and silence of the previous weeks was blown away in a full frontal assault of sound, partying and lunatic driving on that first night. Such an attack on my senses was to be a regular feature of my stay in Barbados. It was not a case of actually doing the partying and driving but it was impossible not to be embroiled in the unceasingly loud Dab music hogging the air and the unflagging 3-tone horns of the buses.

The occupation and development of the Caribbean as a whole has been a tumultuous affair over the years with clashes between the native populations and the European colonial powers shaping political boundaries. The trade in slaves from Africa and their subsequent emancipation have created a diverse cultural mix that is synonymous of the region. Barbados achieved independence from Britain in 1966 and has become an island attractive to both tourists and offshore commercial enterprises. The vibrancy of its past and that of its present is unmistakably reflected in the energy pumping out of the bars, buses and party-boats. The latter refers to the large catamarans and mock pirate ships entertaining cruise-ship passengers with rum, music and cries of 'Are you having a good time?' I grew tired of that question as it was fired incessantly across Carlisle Bay but, as I snorkelled on the wrecks in the company of turtles and walked the fine sandy beach, my answer was always an emphatic 'Yes!'

The arrangement with Jacqui was to meet her in St Lucia at the beginning of March which meant I had over a week to rest, recuperate, and clean *Aluffe* and all her contents before the need to make tracks arose. The mystery of *Aluffe*'s slowing pace in the latter part of the crossing was uncovered when I dived to check her condition underwater. At first glance it looked as if she had grown a beard such were the shocking numbers of gooseneck barnacles growing on her hull. Particularly at her stern and on the trailing edge of the keel there was a thick layer of the critters that had somehow managed to become attached to the boat on passage, oblivious to the effects of the antifoul I had carefully painted on in Nazare less than 2 months beforehand. It was no surprise that *Aluffe* had struggled with that carpet attached. Checking the log impellor I also found 3 more had moved into the minimal space available which would have done nothing for its accuracy. Looking at them closely it was possible to see the delicate intricacy of the fans they spread, tentatively catching food as it drifted past. Clever stuff but they had to go and the most effective way of removing them was to spend a couple of hours scraping a wooden spatula from stern to bow. In the process any remaining antifoul that was of any use was lost, but spending the occasional hour scraping the hull in the warm clear waters of the Caribbean in the future was hardly a price to pay.

Spending over 3 weeks in a state of relative idleness had understandably done little to improve my fitness. Constantly bracing against the rolling motion of the boat was tiring and draining in its own way, but without the opportunity to stretch properly and walk about I felt shaky by the time I made it ashore. My knees in particular had stiffened and become sore from the lack of movement and I was glad for the exercise, even though that caused its own aches and pains at first as muscles and ligaments were woken and forced into action.

I took to walking as much as I could around Bridgetown and the local area, on one occasion ending up in the Barbados Museum. It had an eclectic collection of artefacts that traced the history of the Caribbean and Barbados. As might be expected there was much reference to the slave trade and how from it grew the island states that exist today. I was drawn to the description of the slave ships and the horrific conditions in which they transported between 1500 and 1850 around 14 million Africans across the same waters I had so recently travelled. My cabin floor berth was smaller, in fact, than the space allotted to each slave, but their allocation was still not as big as the average person and was partially shared, so great was the overcrowding. In addition the slaves were permanently shackled, unable to sit up and rarely free to 'dance the decks'. For weeks they would remain, virtually starving, lying together amongst their own excretions, asphyxiating inside the stupefyingly hot ships. It is no surprise that so many, around 12 percent, perished from illness, starvation or suicide, before they made it to the Caribbean sugar plantations. Given the barbaric nature of the trade and its exponents it is sadly of no surprise that there are tales of slaves being thrown overboard alive during storms to lighten the load. It is sickening to imagine such a truly reprehensible trade ever existing and worse being encouraged, and yet slavery does continue in the form of work houses, indebted manual workers, and much of the sex trade.

I thought once again of the early Spanish sailors who would have so welcomed the sight of the Caribbean and cherished their first plunge into the sea. The arrival of the slaves in the years that followed would have been very different and joyless.

I was surprised as I made my way through the Windward Islands that there was not more obvious bitterness from the local people directed at the tragic nature of their origins, particularly on the 200th anniversary of the abolition of the slave trade. There were a few references to me as 'Whitey' although they could never have been read as being deliberately antagonistic but more as a statement of fact, even welcome. Perhaps I was naïve, blind to harsher realities, but I got the distinct impression from my fleeting view of the islands that the local people had largely reconciled themselves of the past and wanted to move forward.

In Dominica, Yellow, a local Rasta, told me that an apology from the likes of Britain, Portugal or Spain was fairly meaningless so many years down the line and would do little to amend the injustices of the past.

He was more concerned about the rise of the Caribbean into a region of prosperity, providing hope to the many poor of a better future with well paid jobs. With the collapse of the sugar industry much of the economic growth on many of the islands came from the production of bananas and other exotic fruit for Europe and North America. Unfortunately, those industries are on their knees today and there is now a greater reliance on tourism and the development of hotel complexes. In this sector the jobs are few and mostly low skilled. Yellow agreed that it was hard to see from where the more meaningful jobs he sought were going to come but was adamant that the Caribbean islands should be freed from the crippling debt repayments that so many of them faced after years of economic support programmes from the wealthy nations. The irony that the people should have attained their freedom only to find their countries shackled by global economics, understandably, grated with Yellow.

Religion, perhaps even more because of the troubled history, runs deep in the Caribbean and not least so in Barbados where the Anglican Church dominates the spiritual scene. Churches and chapels abound along with those of the multiplicity of sects that co-exist on the island. The songs of worship hang in the air on Sundays as the congregations gather for supervision. Spiritual icons and pronouncements are ever present in shop windows, on office desks and plastered across the windscreens of buses. In the UK in the '70's and '80's it was not uncommon to see the names of the occupants of a car displayed in a strip on the windscreen, like 'John – Sandra'. There was a similar practice associated with the minibuses that tore around the island suggesting that the owner was 'Jesus Christ' or 'Virgin Mary'. Sometimes the citations were more descriptive, as was 'Devine Chariot'. There was no doubting the importance of faith to the Bajans and by the speed at which they drove it seemed they were in a hurry to meet their maker. Each to their own, I say, but I question the apparent need to drag a bunch of strangers along as well. I opted to carry on walking rather than squeeze into a heaving minibus emblazoned with 'Next Stop Heaven'.

I eventually wandered over to the Port Authority to clear Customs after the police pointed out my yellow Quarantine flag still flying at the spreaders of the rig. Form filling can be a laboured process at any time and place, and Barbados provided its own subtleties. It was not so much the delay in getting to Customs that was a problem or my failure to provide any additional crew for Immigration to stamp, but Mike in Port Health Authority was very concerned about me having no friends. An offhand quip to suggest as much by way of explaining the solo nature of my trip was, I could tell as the words left my mouth, an open invitation for him to set me straight on the matter. The pausing of his pen, the stiffening of his back and the lifting of his eyes to meet mine all coincided with me registering the very large cross on the wall behind him and the exhortations of the preacher coming from the radio on his desk.

"We all have a friend in Jesus," he stated solemnly and unequivocally.

"That's nice to know, but I meant it as a joke," I replied, wondering where we were going.

Mike, a Seventh Day Adventist as it turned out, didn't get the humour and I was swiftly drawn into something of a debate about the existence of God and the big surprise all us sceptics would get in the fullness of time. He still hadn't stamped my forms when I made my faux pas and so I tempered my argument in case he refused me entry out of spite into what was, I had been reliably informed before arriving, Paradise. For him to suggest I had some way to go before I got there annoyed me when I felt he should have been concentrating on doing his job. Despite his best intentions we ended up agreeing to differ, although he trumped me at the end by pronouncing that I would one day become a great religious leader. It was a kind thought although I sensed a flaw in his logic. He didn't strike me as a betting man, but I told him not to lay any money on it anyway.

Such was the friendly nature of the Bajans and the interest they showed in strangers I did not always have to leave *Aluffe* to meet them, despite being anchored 150 metres away from the shore in 7 metres of water. Relaxing on-board one day I idly watched the swimmers nearer the shore playing in the surf. There were more serious swimmers ploughing their way back and forth across the bay, nearly a mile each way, and there was Trevor. I didn't notice Trevor until he was within a few metres of the boat and my first impression was that he was out of his depth and in some difficulty. His movement through the water was laboured at best and demonstrated more enthusiasm than skill. He raised one arm in a quick wave, sinking a little lower in the water.

"Hello, I'm having a swim," he said. I wondered if his style had been the cause of some confusion in the past and he had subsequently adopted this explanatory greeting to stave off unnecessary attempts to rescue him.

"Is that your boat?"

"Yes, it is." I replied.

"It looks a nice boat." he commented with a slight gasp, the tasks of talking and swimming being difficult to combine. "I'm having a swim. Can I come aboard?"

I had been busy doing very little moments before and was not prepared for company, but the look of pleading from Trevor, disguised as cheery hope across his dark face, banished any hesitancy.

"Of course. Climb up at the back but be careful, it's not very stable." There was no ladder up which a swimmer could climb and some effort and agility was needed to clamber over the push-pit using the Navic for a step. Trevor was not lacking in effort but the required level of agility was missing. I am sure he would have persevered and eventually cracked it but possibly not before *Aluffe* had sustained some damage. After watching nervously some of his early aborted attempts I suggested he try climbing into the dinghy first which was tied to the stern. From there he could manage the step onto *Aluffe* more easily. He agreed to the idea and after a few goes with much huffing and puffing he rolled into the dinghy. Getting from a dinghy onto a boat takes a little getting used to and my guess is that it was all new to Trevor. The light, soft bottomed dinghy did not provide a stable platform and he wobbled precariously as it slewed from side to side. *Aluffe* only added to the troubles as she swayed in her normal fashion. Eventually, as he lunged one more time for the guardrails, I grabbed Trevor's arm and dragged him unceremoniously onto the deck where he lay like a large seal, catching his breath.

Trevor manoeuvred himself into the cockpit and sat in a dripping mass, his copious belly folding untidily over his skimpy swimming briefs. He had a broad unassuming smile and sighed with great satisfaction at having arrived. I offered him a drink and we talked for a while about Bridgetown, the island, jobs and swimming but it was apparent that clothing was of greater interest to him, particularly the lack of it. During the conversation he would make references to the state of his dress and ask me about my wardrobe. He was quite matter of fact about his habit of swimming naked, and asked me how many pairs of shorts did I have? Did I wear pants? My answers were not particularly enlightening but he obviously found the direction in which he was taking the conversation arousing, judging by the stretched fabric of his swimming trunks. Taking a more reserved line when Trevor suggested we would be more comfortable with the removal of his stressed clothing I made it clear that it was time for him to cool off with a swim to shore. If he was disappointed it was difficult to spot as he maintained his broad smile before heaving himself over the rail and into the water, striking out for shore.

Just prior to leaving in January I circulated my plans in an email to friends. Within minutes Matt had replied from London with a buoyant 'See you in Barbados!' His holiday plans to the island coincided with my passage plan and I managed to track down his hotel in amongst all the smart tourism developments blockading the west coast. Arriving at the central bus station in Bridgetown I was set upon by a large number of drivers and 'conductors' all frenetically intent on taking me to their destination, irrespective of whether it cross referenced favourably with mine or not. In amongst the commotion of tooting horns, arm waving and determined shouts I managed to find a bus that claimed to be going in my direction and jammed myself into one of the remaining places. After a few false starts to allow more people to cram into the fast diminishing standing space, the bus eventually roared out of the station trailing a cloud of dust, rocking around the street corners, pressing me and my fellow passengers closer together on each bend.

If nothing else the bus was blessed with good brakes and a very loud music system. It was fortunate that the brakes were good because the driver was very forgetful and only remembered he had them just in time to avoid a number of multiple car pile ups he nearly created along our route. With the throbbing bass beat of the music mutilating most of our senses I can only assume that the police motorcyclist who stopped the bus after it shot over a roundabout and across 2 lanes of unsuspecting traffic did so by visually flagging the driver down rather than rely on his siren.

It turned out that my assumption was wrong in that the bus had caught the attention of the policeman not for any obvious illegal manoeuvre but for having a bum sticking out of the window. The offending article belonged to a German tourist who had taken it upon himself to partially solve the problem of no space by placing a substantial part of himself outside the bus. Whilst ingenious it wasn't legal and we were forced to wait while the German, the driver and policeman had a confab on the pavement. Without wishing to have been uncharitable it would have been appreciated if the policeman had thrown the book at the German and whisked him off to jail because we, the remaining passengers, would have appreciated the extra room in which to breathe. As it was the policeman handed out a caution to the driver and we were left to admire the German's continued genius as he proved something could be found out of nothing by squashing all his bulk back in the bus.

Matt is one of my oldest friends. I think we knew each other before either of us was conceived. We went to the same school for a while and were regular visitors in each others homes. I was very pleased to meet up with him and his wife, Caroline, and their son, Jack, as it provided me with a welcome link to home. Chatting as we walked along the golden sands, the surf rushing to and fro over our feet, I was more able to place my trip in the context of the world in which I had grown up. To hear the simple amazement at what I had done expressed by Matt made me understand more clearly the motivation behind some of the more questioning comments uttered before I left. He is not a sailor by nature and so I moderated his feelings accordingly – the mere fact I had stepped on a boat at all was a leap of imagination for him – but his difficulty in fully comprehending what was involved appeared to mirror that of others.

In describing the trip I tried to give an accurate account of the low times as well as the highs. It was important to explain that my appearance in Barbados was one event at the end of a long line of many others, each of which had contributed to my arrival. Trying to impress upon people that I had not just appeared in a miraculous instant but had made gradual progress to the island over time was difficult, however. Descriptions of the depression and monotony from which I had learnt so much didn't seem to count for much when the norm for most people was to get to

Barbados by aeroplane in a few hours. It was not easy to shake the idea that travelling from the UK to the Caribbean alone in a small boat over a period of weeks was quite mad.

Despite the mixed reviews I was touched by the many messages of congratulations I received. Those, and the efforts I made to downplay the astonishment of the 'How big?', 'From where?', and 'Alone?' crowds, had the encouraging affect of pushing aside the bewilderment I had also experienced when I first dropped anchor in Carlisle Bay. Rationalising the journey to others reaffirmed the logic behind my thinking and the events I had experienced along the way. It was an affirmation I could not really share with anyone else but I became more convinced of the veins of normality that ran through my trip and, subsequently, more robust in the defence of my sanity.

Moving on from Barbados came after a couple of days in the company of *Dart Warrior*, which arrived safely after an uneventful trip from the Cape Verde Islands. Kieran, Maxine and Fontaine were heading south to Grenada for a few weeks, as was *Medley* and her crew, but I had a date with Jacqui in St Lucia, 24 hours to the north-west. As I set off to Rodney Bay I enjoyed the freedom that a boat in the Caribbean offers. With predictable winds to drive sailors across the short stretches of water between the islands, a boat was an ideal mode of transport. I was aware, however, that my pleasure contrasted unfavourably with many islanders who would dearly have loved to have had access to a boat of their own. The ferries were expensive as were the aeroplanes for the poorer families. These official carriers were also quite strict about the transportation of drugs which was a problem for Charlie, aka Mr Cool.

Charlie had found me on the beach in front of the hotel in which Matt was staying. He was local to the area but was clearly not in a position to enjoy the vast wealth on display along the beach front. He lived behind the grand complexes in a small and run down wooden house, and made part of his living by supplying tourists with locally grown dope. There being no demand from me, we chatted for a while about other things. He soon picked up on the fact that I had a boat and immediately he focused on trying to convince me to take him to St Vincent. In fact, there was no need to take him all the way, he told me, because he would arrange for 'some people' to meet us offshore, whereupon he and 'his luggage' would jump ship. His argument that I, as a white man cruising on his yacht, was above the suspicion of the authorities was sound bearing in mind that *Aluffe* was never searched in all my time in the Caribbean. He appealed to me as someone trying to get ahead in a society that could do so little to help him. It was, as he correctly pointed out, a small thing for me and bore no risk, but for him it would signify the deal of the century. There was never any doubt that I would not help him, but my refusal was less to do with a principle of not getting involved with drug trafficking than a fear of getting caught, no matter how remote the chance. I sympathised with Charlie and I was surprised to feel awkward at having to turn him down. Sailing away from Barbados I could see how very easy it would have been to give Charlie a lift, but even if there was no cost to me I did wonder who would pay the price at a later stage.

Crossing to St Lucia was swift with a good breeze behind me and the delights of Matt's ipod to entertain me. I had mentioned to him my failure to carry any music on board and promptly been presented with his sleek black nano. I put up a struggle at first but, inevitably, succumbed to his generosity and my starved appetite for music. The nano was packed with songs and it didn't matter that most had been chosen by Matt's 8 year old son, it was music to accompany *Aluffe*'s rock and roll. Lying in my berth listening to the melodies and lyrics the intensity of distance sailing was immediately relieved, my mind being transported on different wanderings in accordance with the tone of each song. The only drawback was the lack of any charger to go with it and so, having run the battery dry before reaching St Lucia, I was reduced to asking other yachties to charge it until I could find means of my own.

I reached Rodney Bay to the north-west of St Lucia at daybreak and slipped into the marina, unnoticed other than by a large fish that leapt high into the air, eyeballing me for a surreal moment before dropping back into the water. Carlisle Bay is no longer the popular landfall it once was when the annual Atlantic Rally for Cruisers used to stop there. Partly because there is no marina the rally rerouted to Rodney Bay which caters for hundreds of yachts. Having come from Carlisle Bay where there were few other boats anchored with me I was momentarily overwhelmed by not only the number of yachts in the marina but also by their size. The average yacht was in the region of 45 feet with plenty pushing the 70 – 80 foot mark. There was no doubt that boats the size of *Aluffe* were uncommon, as evidenced by the pontoons which were built so high that their underside was level with the top row of her guardrails. My fenders were wasted in the marina with nothing to rub up against and I had to make *Aluffe* secure with a cat's cradle of warps for fear of her slipping under the pontoons with the rise and fall of the tide.

Aluffe's arrival, as people woke, caused little ripples of excitement as she was noticed, dwarfed in amongst her larger cousins. One elder French-Canadian came belting across in his tender shouting and waving madly.

"Excellente, mon brave! It is good to see someone doing it properly." he exclaimed with a large smile.

He nodded his head vigorously and said a bunch of other stuff which I didn't understand but the gist, I gathered, was that he was impressed with my efforts, considering the size of *Aluffe*, and there was really no other true way of crossing oceans. I was beginning to appreciate the sentiment regarding the effort involved but was not convinced it was the only way to travel, particularly in light of the lengths to which everyone else in the marina, including him with his 50 footer, was seeking to demonstrate alternatives.

St Lucia boasts 2 airports situated at either end of the island. The long distance international flights, including Jacqui's, land at the southern one. I made my way down there by minibus after a couple of days preparing *Aluffe* for her extra passenger. Relocating all the foresails and tool boxes that normally filled the forepeak to the starboard quarter berth allowed for the creation of a small and very cosy double bed arrangement. Moving around the boat would require even more care and dexterity than when on my own but the thought of being in close proximity to Jacqui wasn't my primary concern. Time, however, would prove that not all kinds of closeness were good as the Caribbean heat raised the temperature inside the boat to oppressive levels and the desire to avoid physical contact and the heat of company was disappointingly strong.

If I imagined the journey down the length of the island would give me the opportunity to get more of a feel for its environment and even meet some of the locals, in some ways, I was correct. The manner in which this would be achieved, however, depended largely on the style and character of the driver. Initially I didn't know if he had aspirations to graduate to the bus routes on Barbados but I came to suspect he represented the pinnacle to which all other drivers strove to reach. The fact that he wore his sunglasses upside down indicated that he held a different perspective on life to me, and the speed at which he caned his vehicle past slower examples on the outside of bends was matched only by the ferocity of his braking to avoid those coming the other way.

Wedging myself into a corner I watched the coming and goings of the passengers who miraculously succeeded in stopping the bucking bus with barely audible requests to the driver. Others on the road needed only to nod slightly or raise a finger nonchalantly to halt our hectic pace in its tracks. In amongst this storm of screeching tyres and blistering acceleration/deceleration, however, every passenger displayed great calm, indicating an unfathomable nonchalance towards the experience. Even the face of the driver remained impassive despite his manic driving style. I wondered at first if they were all as bemused by the Country and Western tunes blasting from the stereo as I, but settled on a vague theory that relied heavily on the balance of life and the attraction of opposites.

Picking up on the calmness of my fellow passengers I was able to relax and absorb more of the lush and fertile land that is St Lucia as it hurtled past. Banana plantations were common place in amongst the dense forests lining the steep valleys and winding roads. Taking a route that started on the sheltered west coast, we traversed the island to the rugged east coast as we headed south. The many bays and coves we passed by showed the same signs of resilience as those of the cliffs facing up to the Atlantic weather systems remorselessly pounding ashore. It was easy to see why the striking nature of the shoreline was so attractive to the makers of the Pirates of the Caribbean films.

With only a slight hiccup at the immigration desk Jacqui was eventually allowed to enter the country and we settled into a chalet for 4 days on the outskirts of a nearby village overlooking a secluded cove. The change of scene for Jacqui was significant having landed in the warmth of the Caribbean after months of miserable British winter and those first days provided some time to adjust to the strength of the sun.

St Lucia is a very beautiful island and an attractive location for many movies and television programmes alongside the Pirates trilogy. It is also firmly established on the well worn cruise-ship route, each one carrying thousands of relatively wealthy passengers. For their benefit the locals have geared themselves up very effectively to provide short tours to various 'not to be missed' sights of interest. At each of these honey-pots heavily laden stalls selling the same limited range of crafts and clothes at inflated prices crowd the entrances. Local guides volunteer their services for a discretionary fee from their clients who have no idea what constitutes a fair payment that will not distort the local wage structures. This is a common and understandable, some would say vital, trait of tourism in countries of smaller economies and is seemingly fine for the cruise-ship brigade. The Botanical Gardens, at Soufriere on the west coast, were interesting but paying our guide a fee similar to that of the day rate for the average worker on the island for 2 hours work was awkward. It is not that he was not a good guide or we could not afford the rate but it was also the same price I had to pay for some very small trinkets off one of the stalls. Such distortions in the value of goods and services were difficult to appreciate and I suspect some of the locals not able to access the tourist gravy-train think the same.

For those visitors travelling more slowly, as we were heading back to the boat in the north, it is difficult not to get caught up in the nauseating hospitality whirlwind directed more towards those with less time to spare on the many 'Trips of a Lifetime' and 'The 8th Wonder of the World'. Nothing is a trip of a lifetime and the 8th Wonder of the World is overrated, as was the 'Worlds Only Drive Thru Volcano', also at Soufriere, which you couldn't. It left a hollow feeling to see so much effort being put into falsely pumping up certain attractions when the greatest excitement and insight into any of the Caribbean islands can be found by simply getting on a local bus.

We stayed only a couple of days in Soufriere and left feeling a little flat for the experience. Perhaps unfairly, I felt tainted for being associated with the wealthy tourists from the cruise-ships whose brief 'stop'n'shop' tours made me more self conscious of the obvious cultural and economic gap dividing myself from the locals. A 'them-and-us' situation was not something I wished to promote but the opportunity to pass the days chatting idly was missed as time was slipping away for us. Amongst many other things I felt I could have learnt so much more from a local weather forecaster.

"Hey, how do you like the sun in St Lucia?" shouted a smiling man from across the street.

"We like it a lot," we called back.

"That's good but make the most of it 'coz it's gonna snow next week!" he pronounced. There was not much to say to that but laugh and admire the inexplicable beauty of the place.

As our minibus strained out of Soufriere I caught sight of a man walking down the street with a wheelbarrow on his head. It looked a perfectly functional wheelbarrow from where I was sitting and it remains a pleasant mystery as to why he was not pushing it. Entering a village further along the road we roared passed a dusty sign, reminiscent of an English rural scene, reading 'Please drive slowly through our village'. It seemed of all the notices that the village could have put up, the one most likely to be ignored. Perhaps it was a joke or an example of hope.

Returning to *Aluffe*, anchored in Rodney Bay, we did not delay long for fear of being swept up in the deluded hopes of the gathering English cricket fans at the onset of the World Cup. Martinique came as something of a shock confronted as we were by the French and their culture en masse. Stopping first in one of the main marinas, Le Marin, there were charter boats, catamarans and baguettes everywhere. I am probably blind to the excessive British influence on other islands but the extent to which the French have occupied Martinique is stark. I confess I loved it. There is something about the French and their belligerence which is strangely very appealing.

"We 'ave un Caribbean islund, oui, but it will be France. Vive La France!"

Holding the status of an Overseas Department with the necessary thousands of civil servants in attendance, it does carry more than just a few similarities to France despite the expanse of water separating the 2. The language is spoken by the majority of the population and French cars predominate on the smart roads. Modern buses run efficiently through the island and the essence of French style and culture hang in the air.

To maintain the standard of living displayed could not come cheaply on an island that relied, in the same way as others in the Caribbean, on the main agricultural crops of sugar and bananas. That the island benefits from considerable financial support from the central government is undeniable, so much so that I am sure the plaintive cries of the Finance minister far away in Paris could be heard on the beaches of Martinique after being told the enormity of the subsidies being paid out.

We worked our way slowly up the west coast, stopping for days at a time in pretty bays, accompanied by other cruisers and day trippers. In the waters so warm and clear, Martinique served up a daily recipe of snorkelling amongst the shoals of uninhibited silver fish and small groupings of cuttlefish. With the constant exercise I welcomed the return of my fitness, particularly the expansion of my lungs which allowed me to cruise the rocky depths for minutes at a time. The sun was strong, however, and tested Jacqui's rate of acclimatisation preventing us from exploring inland. I was not too keen to stride into the low hills, either, as it looked dry and hard work, something that would not normally deter me. Strangely, though, I didn't seem to mind the idea of the Caribbean softening me up.

With a need to press on in our passage north, we decided to stay a couple of nights in the small marina at Pointe du Bout, across the water from Fort de France, before crossing over to Dominica. The idea was to clean ourselves up and bring some provisions aboard but our plans did not go entirely smoothly. As an Englishman sailing in French waters I was not unaware of the turbulent maritime history and rivalry between the 2 nations. Subsequently, I was determined to conduct myself in a proper seafaring manner at all times if only to keep pressing the claim for British supremacy on the waves. Unfortunately our entrance into the enclosed marina, surrounded by busy cafes and restaurants, almost undid all the good work of Nelson and MacArthur, not to mention that of all those heroes sandwiched in between. Seeing all the other boats in the marina tied stern-to on the pontoons I assumed the line they all had leading from their bows was attached to their anchor. Ordering Jacqui to prepare ours it was only at the last second that I realised the bow lines had been pre-laid by the marina and had nothing to do with anchors. All we had to do was back up to the pontoon, lift a line from the water and attach it to the bow.

Dropping our anchor, apart from being entirely unnecessary, would have most likely created an almighty tangle in the depths and generated howls of derision from the queue of people waiting for the ferry adjacent to our spot. Having just managed to avoid an enormous balls up we gratefully washed and hung out all our clothes in the bright sunshine before the clouds rolled in and the heavens opened.

Rain is short lived in the area and normally a welcome clearing of the air. However, the marina complex had been built on a reclaimed swamp and some of the original residents had not yet departed. The damp environment the rain left behind on *Aluffe* did not persuade the remaining mosquitoes to leave any quicker but rather encouraged them to feast at our, or rather Jacqui's, expense that night. She went to bed an English rose, and awoke a rather irritable cauliflower. For my part I had slept in the hammock stretched out under the thin, and only partially water proof, awning covering the cockpit to give Jacqui more breathing space in the clammy forepeak. A series of rain bursts toyed with my good humour and left behind a palpable tension in the air the following morning.

A late start for Dominica in the morning was more an act of ill-advised flight than a good idea as it meant we were destined for an arrival in the dark at an unfamiliar anchorage. A brisk offshore wind over a flat sea smoothed some of my doubts running up the coast of Martinique and we raised all the mainsail and the large genoa to speed us along. Making the crossing between the 2 islands was a different matter and we bashed into a steep sea and 20 knots of wind almost close hauled. I was quite happy to see *Aluffe* taking on the waves after a period of rest and easy sailing. She was moving well and at a good pace, and I liked the feel of her easy helm but it was difficult to convince Jacqui that I really was enjoying myself as waves occasionally swamped me in the cockpit. The fact that the water was pleasantly warm was of little interest to her as seasickness took hold and conjured up from within her an understandably negative view on life for much of the passage.

As we closed on Dominica so the darkness closed in around us and it was not easy to lighten her mood. By the time we dropped anchor off Roseau Jacqui was at a very low ebb and it took some careful talking to dissuade her from heading home immediately. I sympathised with her on an uncomfortable 24 hours. The combination of mozzies, damp clothes, hard sailing, nausea and cramped conditions on *Aluffe* was too much of a rapid change for her but I could not see the need to pack up there and then. The Atkins family on *Medley*, who happened fortuitously to be at the anchorage, customarily invited us over for a rum punch but on this occasion it was better to settle ourselves and get a good night's sleep.

With Jacqui simmering in the forepeak, I arranged myself in the main cabin, discovering as I did so a puddle of water in the port berth locker. I couldn't see where it had come from in that instant but rather than concern myself with it then I concentrated on mopping it out quickly and quietly. I didn't want to add to the already strained atmosphere and pushed the issue aside in favour of sleep.

How things can so quickly change with a new dawn. As the sun rose over the tree covered hills of Dominica any flagging spirits that remained were banished at the sight of the flat, crystal clear sea. A few yachts lay gently at anchor around us, and the cockerels crowing from behind the shambolic row of small hotels lining the shore appeared to note our new presence. Eating our breakfast, calmly taking in the soothing scene around us, the arrival of Kieran on *Dart Warrior* only added to the enjoyment of the moment. We all gratefully drank that night on *Medley*, happy.

Jacqui and I took the expedient step of booking into the small Titiwi Inn that overlooked the anchorage. The lure of a large double bed, air-conditioning, and a bath was too good an opportunity to turn down under the circumstances. Despite the comforts at the Titiwi, however, there was no chance of abusing them with overuse as Dominica is simply spectacular and demands that one gets out and explores its many walking trails, lakes, waterfalls and bays. The bus system was less predictable than on the other islands we had visited and so we hired a small jeep to explore places like Champagne Beach, so called because sulphurous bubbles rise through the coral to the surface, and Victoria Falls. It is to the credit of the Dominican Tourist Board that Victoria Falls is officially noted as a place of interest where its most appealing feature is the path one has to take in order to get there. I say path but it is really a testing rock scramble through a forceful river which only makes the arrival at the impressive waterfall all the more rewarding. In any other country I would expect a paved 2 lane highway to be cut through the forest before anyone was allowed to visit. In Dominica they are overrun with beautiful natural idylls and take a much more relaxed view. Driving was a pleasure along the narrow twisting roads that carried us across the island, up and down steep valleys that dripped extravagantly with thick vegetation. It seems extraordinary that the island was stripped bare by the catastrophic Hurricane David in 1979 and has since recovered so dramatically.

We attracted some attention on our wanderings although this was more to do with the local fascination with Kieran's dreadlocks than anything to do with us being strangers or my wayward driving. The presence of dreadlocks on a white-man was a big novelty factor it seemed and Kieran was treated with a mixture of reverent comedy and respect by the Rastafarians. Moses, a Rasta and keeper of the Victoria Falls car park, couldn't get enough of Kieran and barely let us leave.

Driving through Scotts Head village, at the southern tip of the island, we came across what I initially thought was an impossibility in the chilled out communities of the Caribbean – road rage. Pottering out of the village I noticed a car with 3 guys weaving erratically behind us. The driver made some abortive attempts to overtake us before managing to draw alongside us on the inside at a junction. Any alarm we might have had was offset at the sight of all the occupants of the car smiling and cheering Kieran. The driver lent out of his window and handed over a small pack of Dominica's finest horticultural produce.

"Give this to the White Rasta, man," before speeding off.

Abstemious to a fault, Kieran sheepishly returned our stares from the back seat.

"This sort of thing happens quite often. It's a bit embarrassing really," he shrugged apologetically.

The island possesses a high and jagged profile underneath the dense vegetation and it was partly due to that and the determination of the resident Caribs not to be colonised by either the English or French that it was only in 1783 that either of the European nations achieved a foothold. Originally, the warrior Caribs had ventured from South America and usurped the peaceful Arawaks from the islands. However, their ferocity was not enough to maintain autonomy on any of the islands and their numbers have dwindled to only a few thousand. The number of pure Caribs is considerably less as a result of intermarriage with mainly the many Africans transported to the Caribbean for the purposes of slavery. Situated in a small enclave to the east of the island the remaining descendents of this predominant race live off their smallholdings and earn money through the sale of baskets and other crafts. We drove through their territory, and I picked up on a tiredness in the air, as if the ancient community was running low on hope, resigning itself to its fate. Taken to its finite end that will be, I suppose, extinction. I felt uncomfortable as a voyeur should but I would later see in Antigua evidence that I was wrong, and the Caribs' spirit and desire to maintain their identity and heritage in a fast evolving world was very much alive.

Roseau, the capital city of Dominica, was vibrant and fun. There was energy and laughter in the busy streets lined with a mixture of clapper board houses and more modern concrete structures. There was a typical focus of activity around the cruise-ship dock with the customary gathering of clothes and craft stalls, along with the touts selling bus rides around the island for 10 dollars a time. Considering the stunning beauty of the island this was a very good price and I would have gladly paid the money for such a trip had we not driven ourselves and walked on a couple of occasions the 2 mile trip into town from the Titiwi. Along the way we were better able to absorb the sights, sounds and smells of everyday Dominican life in a way that would have otherwise passed us by if we only travelled in cars and buses. It all seemed hectic and chaotic at first, mainly because of the carefree attitude of many drivers, steering and parking on the main highway as suited their purposes alone. But, with enough of the universal needs of food, fuel, and leisure being catered for in the small houses and shops along the route it was impossible not to feel warmly attracted to the place and the people. Fishermen fixed their nets by the roadside, while their catch was sold from the back of a pickup rolling down the road to the sound of a Conch shell. Goats and chickens occupied abandoned plots of land as their owners met in doorways and the middle of the street. It was only in the interests of continuing our journey that we pulled up our anchor and moved on to Portsmouth in the north.

Unfortunately, having picked up such a favourable view of Roseau, the second town of Dominica left us feeling slightly cold. It did not help that I had picked up a stomach bug and had acquired the dubious ability to shit through the eye of a needle. Jacqui, too, was affected, although to a lesser degree, but it was clear that *Aluffe* was not our ideal cruise-ship. Space mattered and the constant need to shift sails, kit and food around the cabin in order to find enough comfortable space for us both was proving difficult. Portsmouth, undergoing major road works in the main street and without the colour of Roseau, was unable to provide the lift we needed to our spirits. Our view differed greatly with those of other yachties at the popular anchorage who swore by the place. They pointed to the lack of commercialism, the typically striking vista of unspoilt mountains, and the rotting coasters along the shoreline which lent so much to the hardy character of the place. I could not disagree with them in principle, and their opinions encourage me to return under different circumstances in the future, but at that time the grey skies, illness, lack of space and a rolling anchorage sadly tainted the visit for us.

The time of parting with Jacqui was fast approaching as we stopped briefly at Les Saintes, a small and picturesque group of islands to the south of Guadeloupe. The large island to their north, another French Overseas Department laden with croissants, was Jacqui's final stop before flying back to England. Our time together had been much needed although it had not been plain sailing. We were coming at the trip from different places and there was some understandable difficulty for Jacqui whom I had asked to fit in around my plans into which I was totally immersed. Living on board a small boat had become easy and natural for me but I should never have expected Jacqui to find it as easy. Given a bigger boat and less tasty blood I think Jacqui would have been more able to settle into the rhythm of cruising. It was a sad moment saying goodbye at the airport, knowing that at least 4 months lay ahead of us before we would see each other again, but I think we were both a little relieved that there would no longer be a need to compete for space in *Aluffe*.

One more leg and I would be in Antigua which had always been a target of mine in order to play a part in the Antigua Classic Week. As Jacqui winged her way home the Classic was still nearly 3 weeks away and so I had time to consider the work needed to be carried out on *Aluffe* in preparation for the return trip across the Atlantic. 2 main tasks had been earmarked, neither huge in their own right but each of significant importance.

The construction of a strong cover over the main hatchway to provide extra protection if I ended up beating into head winds was the first task. Travelling east to west on the trip out I had done no upwind sailing but it was obvious that the sliding hatch neither blocked all the water rushing across the deck, nor offered me the option of ventilation and water protection at the same time. I wanted to build a cuddy that allowed me to have the sliding hatch open while still preventing water from entering the cabin. That job, however, would need greater deliberation and a more urgent deadline for it to blossom into existence.

Instead, I concentrated on the other task of fitting a furling system to the forestay. This would allow me to control the size of the sail from the cockpit. It would require a sailmaker to alter the cut of the large genoa as I was not in a position to buy a new one, but it would make the need for me to crawl up to the bow in bad weather almost redundant. Initially I thought getting the new system fitted would pose a few problems in terms of sourcing the parts and finding someone who had the time. I called ahead to the riggers in Antigua but they were unwilling to soil their hands on something so small, especially in light of the rich pickings they had sitting before them in the run up to the Classic and Race week proper.

In the event, a bit of leg work in Guadeloupe from one end of the marina at Bas de Fort to the other, a chance meeting with an English sailmaker, and the waving of some cash brought about almost instantaneous and highly satisfactory results. The problems of changing sails in bad weather on the return leg had been a growing worry for me and others back in the UK who questioned the sense in it when there was a safer option. Most modern yachts cruising today do have the ability to roll one sail in and out as required from the protection of the cockpit. The feeling was that I would be running an unnecessary risk in not having the same.

The extra cost of the system had played the biggest role in my decision to stick with a large wardrobe of 6, mainly old, foresails rather than the convenience of one that could be furled, but I also felt I would be cheating myself of the opportunity to 'do it properly'. The story of an octogenarian who was on his third solo circumnavigation of the world sailing a 26 foot boat without a furling system made the point that one was not necessary and that perhaps I was being a bit soft. However, aware of my relative lack of experience still and wary of the more tricky conditions that could be expected heading home, I opted to play it safe. It just did not seem sensible to set out with those doubts preying on my mind when there was something that could be done about it in advance.

The day before casting off for Antigua, I leant back against the mast, admiring the new labour saving system attached at the bow. Looking about the marina while soaking up the sun that generously warmed all that it reached, there was no doubting mine was a lucky position basking under the Caribbean skies. The UK was apparently suffering at the whim of an atrocious winter and I could be grateful that it was that year of all years that I had chosen to undertake my self indulgent trip. As something that served no greater purpose than personal enlightenment I often wondered how pointless an exercise sailing around the Atlantic on my own was. Escaping from the drudgery of a miserable British winter provided some reason but mostly I settled on the rewards that came from having managed to partially remove myself from the complexity of a modern society. Doing so by living on a spartan boat was like going on a monastic retreat where the decks could be cleared and the mind cleansed of the rubbish that inevitably builds up and clogs the hard drive of one's mind. The whole trip could be seen as taking one big breath, closing one's eyes and then exhaling deeply.

Any danger of drifting off altogether onto a rare plain of spiritual awareness was avoided with the sudden explosion of a motorboat on the opposite pontoon. The driver had been remorselessly gunning the 2 outboards for no more apparent reason that to piss everyone off within a half mile radius. One of them suddenly took to screaming uncontrollably before erupting loudly in a large ball of flame, sending a wave of heat across the marina. The startled man at the controls ran around in circles for a little while before being handed a fire extinguisher by a restaurateur who looked mightily relieved at the surprising turn of events. With the flames dowsed the engine hung limply to the back of the scorched boat while the cause for all the mess scratched his head ruefully from a safe distance.

'Time to be moving on.' I thought, and we left the following morning.

Chapter 8
Classic Antigua

Before dawn on April 5th I motored up the Riviere Salee that runs between the 2 halves of Guadeloupe and pointed north towards Antigua. Leaving the mangroves that lined my path in *Aluffe's* wake we ran before a following wind on a calm sea in the lee of the receding island. A fair wind picked up and we made our approach into Falmouth Harbour by mid-afternoon, finding a suitable place to anchor amongst the numerous other yachts seeking rest and sustenance in the large and protected bay. Falmouth Harbour, like its famous counter part, English Harbour, a short distance to the east, is an attractive destination for cruisers, racers, charters and the super-yachts of the very wealthy.

On the first evening of my arrival and on many others after I sat on the bow of *Aluffe* and studied the extravagant display of wealth presented by some of the finest yachts in the world. They were an awesome presence. Some stretched well beyond the 200 foot mark and their tenders accommodated more space than that offered by *Aluffe*. I watched one gigantic ketch as 4 of its crew manhandled the vast mainsail onto its boom. The extraordinary thing about it was that they appeared as mere dots standing in the boom itself, with room for plenty more. The rigs of these boats towered into the sky making me wonder at the forces that would be at play under sail. There magnificence could be seen in the quality of their build. The paintwork was immaculate, chrome gleamed, and varnish was buffed until it sparkled painfully in the sun. The crews on each of the super-yachts worked tirelessly to maintain the standards expected by their employers. Not far beneath the surface I suspect chaos reigned, as in every organisation in time honoured fashion, but the impression was one of great efficiency.

Watching *Le Grand Blue*, a proper 300ft ship with gold knobs on, I couldn't begin to imagine a life that would require me to want, certainly need, not one but the 2 helicopters sitting on its deck alongside the fully rigged 60 foot yacht. I suppose one of the 40 crew could work that one out for me. It belonged to a world I cannot imagine but I admired it for the extravagance that it was. As for *The Maltese Falcon* I admired it for what it represented. Preposterously long, *The Maltese Falcon* gleams and sparkles like all the other floating palaces. Most significantly she has 3 tall unsupported masts, attached to each of which are 3 bowed booms. Along these booms sails are rolled out. All the sails can be set in 7 minutes at the touch of a button. Resting in the Antigua Yacht Club Marina the masts had been swivelled so the booms were aligned from bow to stern. Each line of booms took the curve of beautiful snakes. Talking to an older sailor on board his classic wooden Bristol cutter I asked him what he made of the unprecedented vessel.

"It's tempting for me to criticise it," he pondered. "It isn't wooden in the tradition of tall ships and everything is electronically controlled. I wouldn't want it but it's modern, the latest thing, and the more I look at it the more it grows on me."

The world of super-yachts is lavish and ostentatious. This was clear for all to see in Falmouth Harbour. It would be easy to dismiss it as an immoral display of excessive riches in a world where thousands each day die from lack of the most basic necessities of life. This might be true but it would ignore the fact that many cogs make this complex world spin and would probably smack of a little envy. To do so would be to miss the fact that boats such as *The Maltese Falcon* represent a pinnacle of human achievement, if only in the small world of yachting. They demonstrate huge wealth, yes, but also unbounded imagination, ingenuity, resourcefulness and determination. These are qualities that are universally recognisable and admirable. The harnessing of those can produce phenomenal results in any arena.

The flip side to the opulence of the super-yachts was the considerably more humble presence of *Gli-Gli*, a 35 foot Carib Indian canoe built along traditional lines in the mid-nineties, and her support vessel *Fiddlers Green*. Owned and skippered by Doug from Australia, the 90 foot *Fiddlers Green* was a solid, square rig, top-sail schooner from the 1930's which he often sailed single-handed, putting my efforts firmly in place. Ambling through the Caribbean, however, he had been slow to come up with a reason why *Fiddlers Green* should not be the support vessel for *Gli-Gli*. Not long after, the decks were stacked high with the belongings and chickens of the Caribs and their families, whilst the rigging dripped with hammocks. *Gli-Gli* was to take part in the Classic Week before embarking on a journey through the Caribbean islands up to Tortola in the British Virgin Islands. She was crewed mainly by a bunch of Caribs from Dominica, their purpose being to visit libraries, museums and schools raising historical awareness of the Caribbean ancestry. Whilst I detected a degree of hopelessness when I drove through their enclave on Dominica I saw, with their bold efforts to bring about some cultural unification within the region, a tremendous desire not to be passed over by modern society. The training of their chickens to crap on the deck of *The Maltese Falcon* moored alongside rather than that of *Fiddlers Green* was a small but spirited statement to that effect.

My arrival in Antigua coincided with that of a large proportion of the Australian population who were gathering, alongside a vocal contingent of English cricket fans, for the forthcoming match between the 2 rival teams. I don't think it mattered too much who won as the competition was still dragging itself through the long drawn out pool stages but there was plenty of banter and ribbing going on in the bars.

I had bought 2 tickets for the game in expectation of a sell out crowd roaring on its stars, but any thoughts I might have had of selling one of them for a profit were banished at the sight of empty seats and people throwing their own spare tickets into the bin. As a victim of another successful marketing campaign I handed my redundant ticket over to the lady checking our entrance. She gratefully took it and told me to look out for her mother in the afternoon. She obviously got waylaid along the way which was a shame for her company would have no doubt made up for a drab affair on the field. Plenty of singing from both sets of supporters raised the atmosphere to a point, but after the English batsmen had scored their final run in the morning there was a collective groan around the ground at the realisation that it would not be enough. The Australian batsmen duly set about breaking down the resolve of the English bowlers in a manner not dissimilar to a boa constrictor squeezing the life out of its helpless prey. The inevitability of the outcome was such that no-one really cared about the result back in the bars, and the evening ended with me having to row a couple of Aussies back to their boat after they had mislaid their dinghy. The temporary loss of a dinghy from the tender-park was not uncommon given the amount of rum consumed on most nights which tended to prompt a state of forgetfulness more than one of outright dishonesty. Invariably any errant tender could be found attached to another yacht nearby or nudging up against the far side of the harbour in the morning. During my stay in the harbour I found myself delivering various strays to their boats on a number of occasions.

Alcohol, and particularly rum, has a prominent place at the table of Antiguan hospitality. Entrepreneurs have very effectively tapped into the thirst and wallets of the partying holiday makers that throng to the island. In the complex of mainly bars and restaurants that make up Falmouth and English Harbours there was a happy culture of hanging out with friends, mixed with the business of the yacht crews maintaining their charges. A persistent buzz of socialising surrounds the place, fuelled by cold beer, rum and cocktails. In the evenings there would invariably be at least one band playing in a bar and a drinks promotion in another. With the impending arrival of the Classic and Race Weeks the ratio of rum to blood swilling about people's bodies was approaching parity with ever more bizarre consequences.

One evening, I found myself swaying gently beside one of the large yachts tied up in the marina. Like many others this yacht had bright lights illuminating the water around the hull. It looked stylish and attracted fish. Mesmerised by a particularly large one measuring over a metre, gracefully slipping through the water, I had an urge to catch it but quickly shrugged off the silly idea. With the rum circulating, however, I had second thoughts and flung myself off the pontoon in the direction of the fish. I missed it, of course, and I can't say it was the cleverest thing I have ever done but it was liberating to act on an absurd impulse without any thought of the consequences.

"I bet that surprised you." I grinned at the startled security guard who helped me out.

"Man, that was a crazy thing to do," he chuckled, shaking his head.

I hadn't meant it to be so but had acted compulsively. Like my trip as a whole, which was a rejuvenating break from the norm, attempting to catch the fish was uplifting if a little meaningless to anyone else. It seemed also to be open to the same degree of misinterpretation.

The revelry continued and I was invited to assist a group of Australians finish off the contents of the fridge on their chartered yacht. The bon hommie was easy going and I gladly embraced it, imagining my life at home to be more austere as each day and each shot of rum crossed my path. If it was more austere, however, it was also healthier. Before long I began to feel the pace of rising early in the morning to avoid the heat of the sun, and being hustled late into the night on the pool tables. I was also tiring of the often one dimensional conversations that follow a traveller – where have you come from? Where are you going? How big is your boat? Are you mad? Etc. With a few days to spare before the Classic Week started I decided to head to the neighbouring island of Barbuda for a break.

With a population of no more than 1500, very little development and off the beaten track, Barbuda is a small, low lying island that is the antithesis of Antigua. It was for me the perfect haven of rest in my April of indulgence. I nosed my way through the coral reefs that surround the island and dropped my anchor in the shallow waters of Gravenor Bay. Each grain of sand below me was clear to see through the crystal water and there was not another boat in sight. The Atlantic, pounding against the shores a little way to the east, had no effect on my sheltered position and for 2 days I hung on the anchor, swimming in the tranquil bay.

Aluffe's hull got another scrub but mostly I swung lazily in my hammock reading. Without any ambient light to compete against their brilliance the bright stars pulled out the stops to remind me of the glorious mid-ocean nights I had experienced and would do so again. Under the circumstances, it was the perfect way to recharge my batteries. It was also the perfect romantic setting for companionship, and I only wished Jacqui had been there to share it with me.

Travelling alone has many advantages that provide for a sense of welcome freedom in a modern world of boundaries, checks, and balances. The pressure of compromise is removed and one has no concern of being bored or boring. In my own company and without anyone to differ I had become the greatest undiscovered comic and a philosopher that would shortly engineer world peace. It was surely only modesty that kept these talents hidden from the eclectic range of people I met on my trip. Their tales were interesting and I enjoyed all of their company's but if there was a fault it was the very fact that they, and I, had the tales to tell. We were all on the move, going in different directions, preventing any chance of continuity and development in our relationships. It is why the arrival of both *Medley* and *Dart Warrior* in Dominica had been so uplifting. I liked them anyway but seeing Kieran and the Atkins again allowed us to pick up conversations without the need for introductions. The purpose of my Atlantic adventure was not to drift with little aim, swilling back barrels of rum, but was a specific attempt to learn and test myself. I had begun to appreciate that doing it in *Aluffe* on my own was of genuine interest to many people and I did not mind talking about the why's and wherefore's that packaged the journey. What I lacked was the company of someone who could recognise and share the truly wonderful experience, someone who appreciated it as much as I. Anchored off Barbuda, lying in my hammock and looking up into an intoxicating night sky I was accompanied by a big hole.

For all the vaguely highbrow musings about the essence of my trip I returned to Falmouth Harbour and got, to coin a phrase, rat arsed. Presenting myself with difficulty at the registration desk the next day I set about accosting any skipper or owner that approached in an attempt to land myself a place on one of the traditional yachts taking part in the Antigua Classic Week. Given my condition it was all a bit of a blur at first but the effort paid off and I ended up in charge of the mizzen of a 100 foot ketch for the week. The owners generously welcomed on board a host of highly qualified extras to assist in the task of getting the stately *Tiziana*, not a thoroughbred racer if truth be told, around the track.

I like to think I played my part as best I could, drawing on whatever competitive skills I had picked up from my dinghy days, but the racing didn't really bother me. Admittedly, using the bow thruster to help us negotiate a mark on a particularly light day did raise an ethical eyebrow or 3 amongst the experienced racing contingent on board but we largely had a great time powering, sometimes wallowing, our way around the courses. In the main the grandness of the whole occasion resonated most with me. In stark contrast to being on *Aluffe* I could stand or take a few minutes to walk the length of the boat. Between the marks people brought me food and iced drinks before I even thought it would be nice, and when the sail needed trimming I pushed a button. It was sailing but not as I knew it.

Simply being part of a big event was, perhaps, the greatest appeal. I had spent a long time in my own enclosed world, and becoming part of something else, something that was bigger, more complex and offering greater variety to that which I had become accustomed, was reviving. It seemed strange that this should be so having appreciated the simplicity and focus of life at sea so much after my escape from the hustle and bustle of England. However, sharing the same goal each day amongst the whole crew, whom I recognised and who recognised me from the day before, bolstered a sense of belonging which had begun to wane. It reminded me of things that I was missing like cooking an apple crumble and diverse conversation with a beautiful woman. Rather than go to a crowded bar I had a strong wish to eat in a smart restaurant in the company of someone who had a range of other interests beyond sailing. I am not saying the people I met on my tour up to that point were single minded but Allie, the stewardess aboard *Tiziana*, was very attractive. Furthermore, talking to her during the intensity of each race I realised she had a lot of interesting things to say about stuff that was refreshingly far removed from sailing. Run off her feet by the guests on board she accepted an invitation to a meal after they had all left but this, sadly, never came about. Both *Tiziana* and *Aluffe* needed preparing for their respective departures from Antigua after the Classic Week and the opportunity passed. I never got the chance to cook an apple crumble either but at least I managed scrambled egg on a proper stove before *Tiziana* headed back to the Mediterranean. The verdict of Chef, a diamond from Brazil?

"This is fucking good! This is the best scrambled egg I have ever tasted. From now on I only serve this!"

I thank you.

What was not good, according to Martine, co-owner of our Classic steed, was my desire to return to England on *Aluffe*. She was baffled enough by the diminutive scale of *Aluffe* and the thought of me travelling, even contemplating travelling, anywhere in the boat had her stumped.

The thought was beyond the bounds of her reason for a long while and, out of genuine concern for my safety, she maintained a constant barrage of generous offers for me to return on the more substantial *Tiziana*. We all agreed that *Aluffe* could be towed without being a drag and could probably even be accommodated on the deck of the larger vessel, but I was equally persistent in my refusals. *Aluffe* weighed about one and a half tonnes all up, whilst *Tiziana* tipped the scales around the 160 tonne mark. Martine's misgivings were largely based around those statistics where she regarded size as having a positive correlation to risk. *Tiziana* was also far more comfortable with its staterooms, armchairs, and fully equipped galley. *Aluffe* had a rather more rudimentary layout in comparison and Martine struggled with the notion that I actually wanted to travel in a boat that represented so much apparent hardship when it wasn't necessary. From her angle I could see where she was coming from but I had long ago accepted the limits that *Aluffe* offered and was not in need of the security or comforts of a larger boat. Either as an attempt to make my life more comfortable or to provide more windage to hurry me along she gave me her enormous sombrero as a parting gift.

Martine's reaction was similar to that of many others, although I suppose she did offer more in the way of a solution to what was perceived as a problem. There was one occasion when she felt she overstepped the mark by calling on her guests at breakfast to support her. I was unconcerned but they all fell behind my desire to see the circuit through. It added to the trickle of moments when I felt *Aluffe* and I were being taken more seriously. Taking umbrage at the more doubtful commentary was never an issue as it served a valuable purpose in raising questions that I needed to answer for myself. Being on the end of votes of confidence furthered the strengthening of my resolve. I had always considered pluck and ignorance to be my key attributes, more so than skill. As I departed from Antigua, however, my perception had altered. I felt a confidence and belief in *Aluffe* and my own abilities that had not previously been there. Far from being just the half way point in the trip, Antigua marked a significant step forward in my journey.

Chapter 9
Wet ride to Bermuda

Despite my greater sense of mental self assuredness I left Antigua in a sorry state, physically run down after the excesses of the weeks before. Small, painful ulcers littered my mouth and the unsightly cold sore parked on my lower lip acted as an appropriate full stop on the whole affair. Joining Nick and Annie, fellow *Tiziana* crewmates, for a blast in their all carbon rocket ship as they prepared for Antigua Race Week highlighted the differences between all our crafts and I could have handled more of that excitement, but nothing else. As it was, I was set on getting to Sint Maartin in a matter of days and was glad when *Aluffe* and I eventually slipped quietly away. Stopping first in Deep Bay in the north-west of Antigua, my attempts at turning over a new leaf were only slightly hampered by an impromptu meeting with Doug, of *Fiddlers Green*, and a friend. A few drinks and not a little dancing in nearby St John's were followed by a desperate paddle back to *Aluffe* as a squall hit me half way across. It was only ever my intention to stop briefly at Nevis and St Kitts but I had always imagined being in the company of *Aluffe* when I did. As the sharp wind caught the dinghy it was a struggle to make headway and there was a moment when I thought we would be parted, leaving *Aluffe* with the unlikely task of catching me up later on her own. Hauling myself aboard after a brief flap I sank into my berth and prayed for some peace and quiet, happy all the while at the variety being thrown my way.

Making tracks the next day for Nevis I watched the approach of a large cruise ship from the south on my port side. Our paths were likely to cross but, after my experiences of so many ships passing close by, I did not assume that she had seen *Aluffe* in the swell.

"Cruise-ship, Cruise-ship, Cruise-ship, this is yacht *Aluffe*, yacht *Aluffe*. Over"

"Yacht *Aluffe*, this is *Caribbean Dream*. Over"

"*Caribbean Dream*, please confirm that you have me sighted off your starboard bow and indicate your course of action to avoid any contact. Over"

There was a short delay before the radio sparked into life again.

"Yacht *Aluffe*, we have you sighted now and will be altering course. Over"

"*Caribbean Dream*, this is Yacht *Aluffe*, thank you for your trouble. Out"

Holding a cup of hot chocolate in the early morning sun I enjoyed the sight of the vast *Caribbean Dream*, carrying its thousands of passengers, bearing away from her chosen course in order to leave the barely visible *Aluffe* at a save distance. There was no question that the ship would alter course once I had contacted her but it was a commanding feeling nonetheless and made up for the obstinacy of some of the tankers I had met.

I slipped round the bottom of Nevis and sailed straight on to St Kitts and settled for a night in the small marina at Basseterre which was also playing host to 4 charter yachts. As evening drew in I realised they were all together as they called over and invited me for a drink on the largest of the boats. It was daunting enough as a stranger to board a vessel which contained 25 slightly inebriated middle-aged men but quite disconcerting when they all looked at me in the same familiar way that said "You're mad."

If I felt nervous I didn't have a chance to contemplate it as their looks turned swiftly into the same old questions in quick-fire succession. They were a good bunch and one of them made an excellent gin and tonic. I was getting good at explaining myself but the intensity of that particular question and answer session led me to revisit 'why me?' Why had I travelled all that way on my own and not any of them? I could explain why I was doing it but why was it such a surprise to everyone else? I like to think that in principle we all have it in us to do anything that anyone else can do, but perhaps, in the face of reality and individual circumstance, this is not the case. There was no doubt that I had met a good many people in the preceding months who had no intention of copying my path. The majority of these lads, taking a week's break from their families, was of a similar mind, but there were a few of them who sat more quietly with what seemed to be more quizzical looks as if nurturing a newly formed idea. Maybe they could see that there was less madness involved than there at first appeared.

Saba, the tiny Dutch owned island, was fascinating for its sheer cliffs that rose abruptly from the sea leaving no space for any beaches. The rocky outcrop offers some excellent diving but what else it provides amongst its tree lined hills and valleys is a mystery as I made only a short stop to get some sleep. Pitching up in the dark provided the shock I deserved although I did not discover the dangerous rocks lurking a few metres from my hasty anchorage until first light when I had to leave for Sint Maarten. I considered what I would have done if the anchor drop had been delayed for a little longer and the boat had struck them. Had *Aluffe* been holed and sunk, swimming ashore would have been easy enough but how simple it would have been to reach any of the distant houses perched high above me was questionable. It is said that the island once had a reputation for producing excellent sailors and, noting the scarcity of sheltered anchorages, I could see why.

Each of the islands I visited had its own distinctive feature. Barbados pulsed with energy, St Lucia flattered the tourists, and Martinique oozed Gallic confidence. Dominica had natural beauty, Guadeloupe natural diversity. While Antigua and Barbuda joined in perfect harmony, Saba was intriguingly isolated. Sint Maarten appeared to have sold its soul.

Sint Maarten, the Dutch equivalent of the adjoining St Martin belonging to France, appears to accept everything and everyone in its headlong rush to embrace any capitalist wealth and development that is going. It has all the energy of Barbados without the administration of the French islands and is in danger of losing the remaining natural charm it possesses. Plots of development show signs of springing up on almost every eye-catching slope. That they haven't actually sprung yet is the only sign of hope that someone at the top of local governance has realised the island's fragile infrastructure stands not a snowflakes chance in hell of catering for such unchecked exploitation. In Simpson Bay Lagoon marinas are being developed at pace to accommodate the ever increasing number of super-yachts and gin-palaces. The main strip running beside the yacht havens, bustles with brightly lit casinos, bars and restaurants, catering for all tastes. Cars and buses travel bumper to bumper along the only road to the main town of Philipsburg which hosts the cruise-ships and the massive range of duty free goods their passengers have come to plunder. Strange to say but it was everything I needed in my final days of preparation before saying goodbye to the Caribbean.

The whole purpose of stopping at the island was to take advantage of the cheap provisions available. Large supermarkets catered for my interest in stocking up with a greater variety of foods for my return trip than that with which I had travelled out. The remaining tins of squid and Portuguese tripe I offered to the local guys working on the boats in the marina and were gladly taken away. It was good food but the quantity and lack of variety had been too much.

The permanent fix I carried out in the Canaries on the port shroud plate turned out only to be temporary and needed another seeing to, as did the electrics which were suffering from a dying domestic battery. With many of the regular maintenance checks completed I still needed to build the protective hatch cuddy, and did so in 2 days with the final deadline looming. Using some plywood templates I had cut in Antigua I took full advantage of the dry, sunny conditions to wrap them in glass fibre and epoxy. A couple of coats of bright orange paint gave it the final touch before I bolted it securely over the hatch. The space available to get in and out was more restricted but I soon developed a technique which became second nature and difficult for me to explain to anyone else at the same time.

With her new ocean trim attached *Aluffe* drew even more stares and comments as even the casual onlookers got the immediate impression that something different was going on. Placed near the largest yachts money can buy and the many others clearly designed for and intent on long distance voyaging *Aluffe* always looked minimalist and out of place. Taking her out of the lagoon to scrub her bottom one day I passed through the short and narrow channel leading to the open water. Adjacent to the channel is the Simpson Bay Yacht Club which is always busy on a Friday afternoon. The bar was packed as usual with yachties of all calibre and extraction exercising their right to pass judgement on all the boats passing back and forth. I wasn't paying much attention at first but as I pottered by, sandwiched between a large luxury catamaran and a motor yacht, my audience stood and starting clapping. With the Red Ensign flying from *Aluffe*'s stern, the St Piran flag of Cornwall below the spreaders, and her high visibility cuddy, the members twigged my trans-Atlantic intentions and apparently felt moved to express their opinion. It was a different approach to making me feel embarrassed but the attention wasn't unwelcome, and I waved back. I am as susceptible as the next man to having my ego massaged and on this occasion it was another valued boost to my resolve as the time for tackling the tricky passage to Bermuda drew ever closer. A couple of days remained before I would put myself to the next test in the variable waters that stretched north from the Caribbean up to the eastern seaboard of the United States.

Since my arrival in Barbados I had been checking the progress of the 2 rowers, Graham and Bhavik, on the internet. Bhavik had set off first, about a week after I left, and was followed by Graham a few days later. Their progress was, as expected, much slower than mine although Bhavik was experiencing rudder problems that forced him to do more drifting with the current than rowing. Both of them were hoping to arrive in Antigua and it was becoming clear that Graham, his experience making up for the woeful dynamics of his bucket of a boat, was going to make it across first. With only a hundred miles to go he looked likely to land at around the same time I was due to head north. It was a shame that I could not be on the beach to greet either of them but, as I monitored Graham's progress from the vantage point of a bar in Sint Maarten, it became apparent that he was not going to reach Antigua at all because of adverse weather pushing him north. He later reported hearing the waves breaking on the reefs surrounding Barbuda and had to work hard to keep out of harms way. I watched, amazed, as Graham closed on St Barts. If he missed that French colony he couldn't help but bump into Sint Maarten.

My excitement for Graham at his impending achievement tweaked the interest of other sailors and residents in the marina. A high speed catamaran called *Garfield* was put at my disposal and I, in the company of 4 others, was soon bouncing across the sea in search of him, somewhere off St Barts to the south. There was no question of leaving for Bermuda when he was so close to an epic goal.

Communicating with Graham's shore team in the UK we were able to establish his general whereabouts but I still doubted we could locate the tiny *Puffin* in the large swell that had set in. Needles and haystacks came to mind, but find him we did, sheltering in a bay wondering where to land. It was an extraordinary turn of events and I found myself screaming congratulations at him as he gratefully gulped the beer we handed over. He had rowed nearly 3000 miles in 100 days, during which time he had celebrated his 60th birthday.

He followed *Garfield* to St Jean on the east coast where he stepped ashore and promptly fell over in the surf, his wasted legs unable to hold him. This was no surprise after so much time at sea and no surprise also that the many words he had stored up over that period gushed out unabated to the intrigue of the small crowd that gathered around him. He continued to talk, almost without drawing breath, at the mayor of Gustavia, to where *Puffin* was towed, and at all the fascinated bystanders gathering around his 16 foot boat once it was safely tied up to the quay. He became quite the celebrity in the millionaires' paradise. The mayor was so moved by Graham's unexpected arrival in the harbour, which coincided with that of *Gli-Gli*, he put him (and me by virtue of hanging very tightly onto Graham's coat tails) in a plush hotel, all expenses paid.

Not surprisingly many of the people who witnessed Graham's arrival questioned his sanity but in doing so failed to grasp the extent of his preparations. This included the wealth of experience gained in the course of 3 previous successful Atlantic rowing trips. He also meticulously researched the behaviour of *Puffin*, as described in the recovered journal of its original unfortunate crew. For Graham to have woken up 101 days before and deciding to row across the Atlantic would have been insane. He didn't, of course, and his remarkable crossing can be seen as far more calculated and deserved as a result.

The excitement surrounding the landing of Graham and *Puffin* at St Barts had to be put aside shortly afterwards as the weather was favourable for my departure to Bermuda. A steady south-east wind looked set to blow for the next few days and I didn't want to miss out on the opportunity to get a good start. Ahead lay nearly 900 miles of sea offering conditions and sailing that would be less straight forward than anything I had encountered since leaving La Gomera. Whereas there was a strong degree of predictability about the trade winds that had blown me to the Caribbean they would only help me part way to the tiny island. I had been told by many hardened maritime sages to expect steady winds from the south-east for the first few days before a period of calm that could precede either more calm or strong winds from any direction. The first of the tropical storms had been registered along the eastern seaboard of America, accounting for the loss of 4 lives from a yacht that had left the Caribbean the week before. I was timing my passage to match that of the perceived wisdom, but the stretch of water I was crossing was notorious for throwing itself, and any boats on it, into confusion.

Many boats leaving the Caribbean for Europe take a north-easterly route at first in order to pick up the currents and winds that will traditionally be of greater assistance to their passage. The tiny island of Bermuda, only 21 miles long and one mile wide, lies not far off this course but still far enough away from the useful wind and current to be seen, more often than not, as an inconvenient stopover. I, however, after the troubles I had had with solitude previously, wanted to keep the legs home as short as possible and so had no thoughts of missing the island. A 10 day passage followed by one of less than 3 weeks to the Azores suited me better than one direct leg to the European islands that could take almost a month. That was not my style and besides, it was there. To get so close and not to have a sniff seemed a wasted opportunity.

As I cast off from the marina in Simpson Bay Lagoon a small group gathered to make sure I didn't change my mind. Graham had come over from St Barts and was joined by Bruce, skipper of *Garfield*, Tom, Morgan, and Gary, the latter 3 each with a boat to sail somewhere. The chances of seeing any of them again bordered on the minimal but, as is the way on the travelling circuit, it was a bonus to have found their friendship. I knew I could call on them if I did pass their way in the future, and they on me if they ever turned up in Cornwall. I motored away from the pontoons, pausing only to speak with another Cornishman, Mike, who was heading back to the UK, via Bermuda, in his heavy 26 foot catamaran. I envied Mike the space he had on board but preferred the speed and sailing qualities of *Aluffe*.

"When are you off, Mike?" I called.

"I think in a few days time when there is better weather." I wasn't too concerned whether he was implying that my interpretation of the weather charts was incorrect as I had long believed, since I first met him in Dominica, that Mike was very meticulous with his planning to the point of being over cautious. There is no fault in that but sometimes you just have to go at the expense of perfection.

"Ok. I should be stopping in Bermuda for a few days so will hopefully see you there. Have a good passage."

The weather was overcast, hot and sticky, but the wind was a steady 15 knots from the east-south-east pushing me quickly away at the start of my homeward journey. It is always difficult saying goodbye, despite the excitement of all that is to come, and it took me a little while to get my head around the fact that there would be no more conversation, beer and restaurant meals for a little while. I was back into solo sailing mode where meals would be cooked on a rocking, single burner stove and eaten straight from the pan. Thirst would be satisfied by rationed water supplies and a daily mug of hot chocolate, while I would have to rely on books and my ipod for entertainment. I had given up trying to learn the harmonica a long time before but would occasionally bring it out to soften the more noisy occasions. Just so long I didn't get ahead of myself and try playing tunes I found the more gentle harmonies quite soothing.

Within a few hours I was back into the swing of things mainly because *Aluffe* was belting along under the favourable conditions. I took the helm at first to help me get back into the groove but soon handed the responsibility of driving over to the Navic which, with my greater appreciation for getting the sails balanced, managed well. I rarely hoisted the entire mainsail, preferring to keep a conservative reef in, and, with the new furling system performing as well as it said it would on the box, adjusting the foresail was a simple and swift operation. In the first 24 hours we covered 130 miles which was the best start I could have hoped for. Unfortunately, while the sailing was excellent, settling into an efficient domestic routine was not without mishap.

It is not uncommon for male sailors to be lost overboard whilst caught in answering a call of nature. To prevent this from happening to me I used a 5 litre water bottle as a temporary holding tank. This meant that I did not have to lean precariously over the side, wrapping a leg around one lower shroud and jamming up against the other for support, whilst concentrating on the fiddly bits. It also allowed me to satisfy my needs 'indoors'. That first night saw me needing a pee and so, in the dark, I pulled out the bottle. With *Aluffe* barrelling along and being tossed about it was no mean feat to brace myself over the cabin floor. Fast approaching a point of no return I searched for the appropriate position with my business end and relaxed. I had been holding out for the right time for a little while and so it was a very enjoyable moment as the pressure was relieved.

Perhaps it was because I couldn't hear any noise of liquid running into the bottle that alerted me or maybe it was the warm patch developing around my knee, but I soon realised that all was not as it should have been. Despairingly it dawned on me too late that I was relieving myself through the handle of the bottle and not the open neck. There are relatively few pleasures available to the solo sailor and having a much needed pee is one of them. Not only was the moment spoilt but so was my sleeping bag on which I had been kneeling.

'Finish what you've started,' is an admirable piece of advice and one which I wish I was more able to follow as a rule. However, spraying my warm, dry and clean sleeping bag with urine was something I wished to stop desperately, but to shut the tap off at the best of times is not an easy thing to do and one that I had evidently yet to master. A growing panic began to affect my coordination and it was not with panache and flair that I eventually managed to redirect my aim into the bottle. I did the best I could to wash the soiled area in fresh water before hanging it out on the rail, hoping that no waves or rain would make the situation worse. Curled up on a blanket later I took some comfort from the fact that no-one was with me to witness my inaccuracy and it would be my secret for evermore.

The wind picked up even more in the coming days and was joined from time to time by periods of hard rain and slashing lightening in the distance. *Aluffe* made good speed through it all, bucking and plunging through the building waves without too much concern as she was showered with spray. I read and cat napped to pass the time while *Aluffe* got on with the business of getting wet at the helm.

On the second morning, while sorting out the mattress which I put on the cabin floor to sleep on, however, I was curious as to why the floor and the underside of the mattress were wet. Everything had to be dried first before I started shifting kit around the small space available in search of the cause. Once that was completed I lifted the cabin floor and saw the bilges were full of water. There was no immediately obvious reason for this but my inclination was not at first to worry as we were clearly not sinking and still sailing fast. I noticed some wet patches resting on the port berth on the leeward, and therefore the downward, side. I looked inside the large port berth locker and swore under my breath at the sight of all the provisions, previously stacked neatly in there, swilling about in a few bucketfuls of water. We may not have been sinking and we may have been sailing fast, but we were definitely taking in water. The main problem was I didn't know from where.

I dipped my finger into the water and put it to my mouth. It was salty meaning that it was not a case of broken fresh water bottles and confirmed that the problem was going to continue until I found the source of entry. I needed to establish how big the problem was first by getting a clear idea of how fast the water was coming in and so baled out the locker and cleared the bilges. I could not work out in my head how it was getting into the boat, but getting in it certainly was at a rate of about 10 litres an hour. Checks of the prop flange, the keel bolts, and the troublesome shroud fittings did nothing to remove the veil of mystery or my growing concern. With the boat bouncing about so much it was not easy to carryout the most effective search but I managed to check all the lockers and bulkheads, even dismantling much of the galley to check there was no ingress from the starboard side. Wet areas discovered under the forepeak indicated a possible point of entry and I studied the log impellor and depth inducer which were fitted through the hull in that area. I couldn't see how they would be able to let that quantity of water through, but the movement of *Aluffe* prevented me from either discounting my suspicions or pinpointing the cause. There was little more I could do in the 36 hours after I discovered the water but monitor the situation, ponder on the reasons why, and consider my options.

Turning back was not something I wanted to do. Apart from meaning a long beat back into the steady weather we were already finding fairly intense, it would throw all my plans of getting around the Atlantic into disarray. If there was a major problem waiting to happen then time and money would have to come into play and the chances of achieving my goal would be threatened. I found myself in a situation where I was for a while more concerned by the longer term outcomes than I was with the immediate problem which should have been the clear priority. Thankfully, my focus soon returned to the job at hand and I decided to wait for the weather to subside before turning the boat inside out. It was a clear and logical decision in which I had confidence, but not far beneath the surface was a tension that reflected the pressure of being alone in a leaky boat heading further away from the nearest point of safety.

"There is some dirty weather to the north-west but you should continue to get the same weather for the next couple of days, with the wind backing further east on Friday." Dad was keeping me updated with the latest weather forecast and I was relieved that conditions were not going to worsen although, listening to the water sloshing about in the locker, I might have preferred some calming of the sea.

"That's ok. I'll keep plugging on then," I replied, my voice wavering slightly.

"How is everything? Are you alright?" Dad had always had his reservations about me sailing back in *Aluffe* and he was alert to the hesitancy in my voice.

"Yeah. Everything is fine, although…" I paused as I felt the words catch involuntarily in my throat, "….we're taking on some water and I can't work out where from just now. It isn't a problem." I added at the end, hoping to allay any fears that Dad might have.

In fact, having told Dad of the problem, it was quite a relief no longer to have to try and suppress the news, even to myself. The information was out in the open now and being shared to some degree. What was a problem suddenly became no more than an inconvenience as I regularly emptied the water when I would have preferred to be sleeping. It also galvanised me into searching more thoroughly for the offending entry point when conditions became slightly calmer. Still, however, the answer remained hidden. Water breaking over the forward hatch was finding its way through the poor seal, but it was not enough to be considered culpable, and I stuck the whole hatch down securely with some marine sealant. I eventually decided that whatever the problem was it could wait until I got to Bermuda. My destination was only a few days away and if I had to bale out all the way, well so be it.

I had in my mind a story told to me about Pete Goss and another Marine arriving in New York after a trans-Atlantic race in a state of exhaustion. From an early stage in the race their boat was taking in water and their electrics also failed leaving them to hand pump most of the way across. I would have a fraction of the distance to cover and I didn't see the occasional mopping up session as much in the way of comparison.

In the first 4 days we covered over 500 miles. It was hard going but I was ecstatic at the rate at which we were closing on Bermuda. There had always been a slight risk attached to making this leg as the weather was variable enough as to be unpredictable. I had no substantial complaints in those first few days and my mood carried over when the wind did die away and I was forced to run the engine. I could have sat out the calm and waited for more wind but I was discovering that, much as I loved sailing, I was not a sailor's sailor. Confronted by a calm patch and with enough fuel on board to carry me roughly 200 miles I was not slow to turn to my metal friend. Putting the helm in the charge of the new auto tiller bought in Sint Maarten, I was more freely able to tidy the boat and whittle away at the long list of maintenance jobs. In my investigations I had fathomed out that the water leak only occurred when waves were breaking over the boat and so I was forced to wait until more suitable weather conditions arrived. When it did I vowed to be ready.

On a gently lifting but otherwise flat sea I directed *Aluffe* a few degrees to the east of Bermuda. I wanted to get to the right of the direct course in an attempt to be favourably placed when the forecast north-easterly winds filled in. They took a while and I was mighty glad when they did after 33 hours. My head was thumping with an enormous headache, much as I should have expected, eating, sleeping and shitting as I did 4 feet from the running engine. Any frustration I felt at being pushed too far to the west by a wind containing more north in it than expected was offset by the easy sailing. The wind continued to back over the following 24 hours before veering clockwise and strengthening. This had been anticipated when I witnessed a brilliantly vivid red dawn across the sky, heralding heavier weather, the day before. I reduced sail to 2 reefs in the mainsail and about half the genoa but this was still too much as the wind continued to build, provoking the sea into creating tall steep waves that crashed into *Aluffe*'s bow in quick succession. Water broke over her decks as she tried to pound her way through but, being so light, she was finding it hard going. The waves were increasing in stature all the time and I lay on my mattress, trying to read the messages she was sending me through her motion. I wanted to press on as directly to Bermuda as possible, but was wary of over-exerting the boat. *Aluffe* had not faced a sea like this head on before and she was going into it too fast. Much of the time she would rise and fall with the waves, slicing up their face and hissing down the back. All too regularly, however, she would meet a sharper wave which would force her up at a steeper angle, lifting half her length clear of the water as she tipped over the peak. The wave would move swiftly on leaving a deep hole into which she would fall with an immense bang, shaking the rigging and me badly. It possibly felt worse than it actually was but it encouraged me to slow *Aluffe* down by shortening the mainsail further still to 3 reefs, and by rolling the foresail in until it more closely resembled a handkerchief. To try and reduce the jarring impact even more I bore a few degrees off course. Under those conditions we inched our way towards Bermuda making no more than 2 knots over the ground. *Aluffe* impressed me with her solidity amongst a very turbulent sea and my confidence grew.

Water started pouring in again and this time, by clearing out the forepeak entirely, I was able to see what, deep down, I had always suspected. Every time I had dropped anchor I had noticed a large gap that surrounded the redundant water tank pipe that descended from the deck on the port side, through the anchor locker and into the boat. As waves broke over her, particularly when she was on a starboard tack, water found its way into the anchor space. This is not a problem in itself as there is a small hole within the locker to allow water to drain out, but some of the water was easily finding its way through this additional gap. From there it flowed down the length of the boat and collected in the bilges and port berth locker. There had been little opportunity to discover the fault before as much of my sailing had been in good, downwind conditions when little, if any, water broke over the boat. It was, however, clearly the source of the water I had chosen to ignore after crossing to Dominica and so, feeling the idiot that I was for ignoring the obvious for so long, I turned the boat onto port tack and hove-to.

Grabbing a roll of sticky tape and sealant I wedged myself into a safe position on the foredeck and fashioned a temporary repair. The royal blue waves were approaching 5 metres in height and the crests, shimmering in the sunlight like Medusa's serpent hair, threatened to tumble forward dangerously. It was the short distance between each of them, however, that made the conditions more lively and the foredeck behave like a fairground attraction. Adding to the scene was the wind impatiently muscling past the game *Aluffe*, holding her own in this muddle of nature. It was a rugged sea and the intensity of its wildness gave me a burst of adrenalin, making me breath deeply and my pulse beat solidly with excitement. Such were my heightened emotions I felt what must have been masochistic joy at breaking my little toe on a cleat making my way back to the cockpit. I felt a lot of pain as well. It really, really hurt.

Aluffe was pummelled for nearly 60 hours before the wind began to ease, by which time Bermuda had slipped into view like a bright silver beacon in the evening sun. The waves, if anything, became more aggressive as the pattern, previously held by the stronger wind, broke up. *Aluffe* positively jumped off the back of one wave and I had time to picture her in mid-air as she literally dived into the valley below her. My teeth were left vibrating in my jaw as she slammed her full weight down onto the water before piling into the next wave. I didn't like pushing her beyond the limit but, despite those knocks, she remained sure footed and seemingly above it all. It was a growing pride in her tenacity that I felt as we neared the end of our eventful passage. It made me think pityingly of Mike in his catamaran facing the same weather somewhere further back along the track. His boat would struggle to make headway in these conditions and I suspected he would just have to sit it out.

Our entry into St Georges was ultimately delayed until early the following morning by the highly efficient, but cautious, Bermudan coastguard whom I contacted on the radio as a courtesy. Having stripped *Aluffe* and I of all our details barring my inside leg measurement, it proceeded to questioned the wisdom of negotiating the well lit entrance channel at night. I was too tired to prove a point if, by doing so, I was going to give them kittens and so hung around the entrance until first light. Eventually, with the rising sun, we motored through the narrow Town Cut into the still lagoon and tied up alongside the Harbour Office. I clambered up the high wall and staggered onto the jetty, reaching out to a pillar for support. The 10 day passage had taken a lot out of me and my body craved for sleep. It was duly obliged after I had been through customs and found a berth in the local sailing club marina. Making good use of all the washing facilities, it was not long before I and all my drying clothes were to be found draped around the spirited *Aluffe*, soaking up the warmth found in the air of Bermuda.

Relaxing in a sunny meadow after a hard 18 day crossing from Bermuda to the Azores.

MC Donnacha (seated on cuddy) directs proceedings at the pre-departure origami party, La Terciera, the Azores.

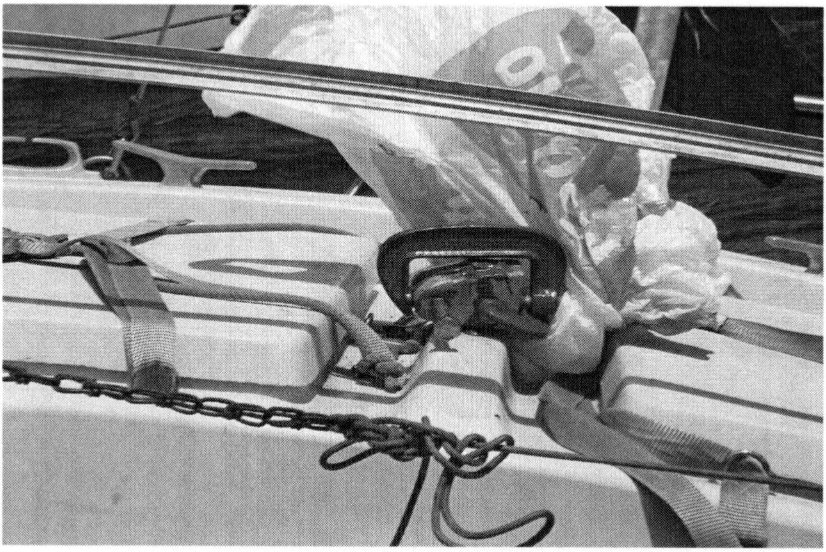

The tiller stock under repair on passage to Spain. A combination of liquid metal, clamps, and 30 hours hove-to saw us home.

With Kiwi brothers Jon and Paul heading to La Coruna, Spain, having the time of my life.

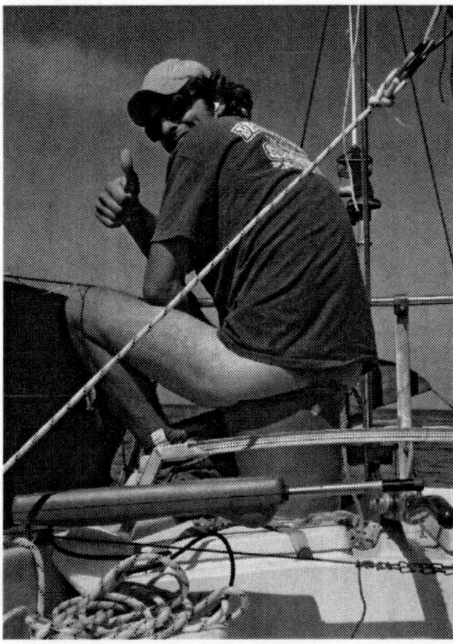

A close eye was kept on the remaining bucket after Paul's earlier error of judgement.

A tangle of warp and fenders await to be thrown over the stern approaching the Western Approaches into the Channel.

On my own or with company it was always a bonus to get the spinnaker up.

Arriving in Fowey on 29th July 2007, all fit and well.

Our mark painted on the harbour wall at Horta, the Azores.

Chapter 10
War and peace

Bermuda is distinct for its precision and sense of order. Located hundreds of miles from the east coast of North America the island has managed to preserve a cultural identity that is very British in a characteristically colonial sort of way. That it should reek of insularity is odd in that immigration and emigration have been important features of the island's history and, in its modern guise, it boasts a strong international dynamic. Both the Portuguese and Spanish made tenuous claims of ownership before England grabbed it for herself as a strategic outpost with the escalation of the American War of Independence. Slaves from the Caribbean, and immigrants from Asia and Europe, particularly the Azores, have created a diverse culture, but it is very much the etiquette and formality of the British system that pervades and binds the current society together.

The cleanliness of the streets mirror the charm of the white roofed buildings and the politeness of the people they connect. If ever a place followed a code of conduct it is Bermuda where nothing appears out of place and everyone knows theirs. With only 21 square miles in which to squeeze a growing population of 65,000 such respect for tradition and form is probably no bad thing. Living on Bermuda is a bit like living on a boat where everything has its place for a reason. Move something and the only thing anyone can see is the imminent collapse of the way things should be, creating disorder and tension. Everything in Bermuda is in its place and 'just so', but an unfortunate consequence is the slight whiff of repression that hangs in the air.

There is evidence that the traditional standards are being shaken up, however, as the political stage changes with an ever more diverse population, and the global re-insurance market sets out its burgeoning stall in Hamilton, the capital city. The demise of the knee length shorts and long socks dress code is unlikely to result in much wailing and tears, but the town of St George's, pickled as a World Heritage Site, represents a set of values on the island that would be shameful to lose altogether.

The passage from Sint Maarten had been one of attrition and I was shattered. The conditions had affected my appetite even more than was normal during a passage. Displaying a full set of ribs and dark patches under my eyes, putting on weight and catching up on some hard earned sleep were the limits of my agenda in the first days after my arrival. *Aluffe* deserved a thorough clean and I needed to carryout a proper fix of the water leak. The trip to the Azores demanded another look at the stowing of gear to ensure I had to hand all that I might need in a hurry. Each passage undertaken gave me another insight into what was important for me and to the efficient sailing of the boat. All the boat management issues would have to wait, however, while I attended to myself and slept. Sleep, on the whole, is a rather dull activity, but any tedium I might have endured was avoided by my timely kidnapping.

Matt, he of the generous ipod, had commanded his mate in Bermuda, Greg, to look after me if and when I arrived at the island. To chuck orders around seemed to be a common attribute amongst Matt and his friends because I woke early after my first night's sleep to find an email from Greg telling me he was on his way to take me out. When he arrived he was true to his written word.

"Are you William? Hi, I'm Greg. This is my wife, Molly. Is this your boat? No way! That's small. We're taking you out."

"Hi, I'm William." I replied blearily, already a bit behind the pace of the day.

Under different circumstances I would have probably explored Bermuda as much as I wanted in a little over a day and not really taken my mind off the small matter of the imminent 3 week passage to the Azores. A few days rest on the pink, sandy beaches, and snorkelling over the abundant coral reefs would have served me well. But, in the company of Greg and Molly, I was treated to a flavour of Bermuda I would have otherwise never had the chance to enjoy whilst getting a guided tour of the tightly packed island. The tour didn't take long even though the cars are restricted to 20 mph along the only main road, but they personalised the route with their stories of events and people important to the island. Greg, one version of a successful Delboy Trotter living in paradise, delighted in dragging me around the island as he conducted his varied business affairs. Much because of the keenness of Molly and Greg to play the generous hosts I ended up fondly attached to the qwerky island, them, and their friends, whom I would have been the lesser for not meeting.

Invited to make myself at home in theirs I couldn't deny myself the chance of living ashore for a few days amongst the soft chairs, glossy books, and well stocked kitchen. Having been thwarted in Antigua I took my chance in Bermuda to gratefully cook a large apple and plum crumble. It was a moment of earthiness surpassed only by the luxury of the large double bed which bore my dreams for 12 straight hours.

Just as the comforts of home were novelties for me, so I felt I was something of a novelty to many of the people I came across during my stay. This I found quite strange as Bermuda is surrounded by the sea and sailing is part of her tradition, but it did not dilute the waves of questions thrown at me during the evening hours of a beach party. I was still quite worn out and getting tired of the unbounded amazement and disbelief expressed at my journey. There was a lot of praise for my endeavours but I felt my inquisitors were getting the wrong impression of me. I fully appreciated that bobbing about on the high seas in a small boat was not for everyone, but the apparent resistance of those questioning me to accept that it might be for someone, particularly me, was beginning to grate. The lack of time and other party distractions were factors in my emerging frustration at never managing to explain myself fully before we had to part. The result was a tendency for people to see me as a one-off hero and adventurer tackling danger at every turn. If I met one of those I would be pretty amazed too, but the reality was I came from a very similar background to them and differed only because I had selfishly thrown caution to the wind to follow a very well worn path around the Atlantic. The idea that such a difference was as mind-bogglingly awesome (and mad, obviously,) as some of them made out was difficult to swallow.

I was relieved towards the end of the evening when one man, whom I had met a few days previously, turned to me and offered, thoughtfully, "You know, I was a bit quick to call you mad before, but really what you are doing is very interesting. It makes me wonder if I shouldn't try something similar." Having grown weary of trying to convince people that I was perfectly sane, I welcomed his admission that there might be some mileage in pushing one's boundaries.

Spending a lazy Sunday with another of Greg's friends and her 3 children the following day was also a respite. They were all very interested in *Aluffe* and the route I was taking, asking lots of questions, but talking under those easy circumstances was a far more enjoyable and positive experience. As active sports people themselves, they accepted my motivation and were keen to know more about how the project had come together, almost as if they were banking the information for future use on a project of their own. We went for a sail on the lagoon which made a refreshing change as I was able to demonstrate the practicalities of fitting inside and the workings of *Aluffe*. By that stage of my trip I didn't need to be told how crazy I was, because it wasn't true. I needed some understanding and approval, and these I was lucky to find.

In fact, amongst the sailing community in particular, I had noticed a change in the general attitude towards *Aluffe*'s circuit. At each stopover I had always been indulged with compliments for my efforts and it was often suggested, wrongly, that I possessed oversized, even metallic, balls. But those compliments were still tainted by the opinion that I was out of my mind. Gradually, as we progressed, this perspective altered until, with around 6000 miles behind us, the sailors in St Georges were not in a position to question my motivation or the suitability of *Aluffe* so easily. A number of sailors had suffered the same meteorological thrashing that led up to our arrival in Bermuda. It had been a rough experience but *Aluffe* had come through unscathed, which was more than some of the larger boats tied up alongside could claim. Gear failure and crew injuries were reported and, worse, there were boats still at sea unaccounted for. It highlighted the dangers that we all faced at sea but gave me renewed faith in the strength and qualities of a small boat in big seas. As a light boat, *Aluffe* rode more easily with the waves and did not fight the powerful natural forces pitching in against her, as a bigger boat driving to windward might. We had bounced about a lot, but I was grateful for that rather than suffer the doubts consuming one sailor who was packing his bags in tears in readiness to fly home.

"It was terrible. I'm getting older and I can't do it anymore. I had my 80 year old father with me in a boat that couldn't cope with the conditions." He paused as the words stuck in his throat. "I don't ever want to face a 20 foot wave again." And with that Tom, from Carolina, headed off for the airport leaving his boat for a delivery crew to bring back at a later date. He had obviously received a big fright and it was probably quite easy for him to curtail his immediate plans. I wished him well and hoped that it would not be long before he climbed back on the horse.

Perhaps it was because of his experience and the considered comments of other seasoned sailors, alongside the more heedless ones of the sceptics, that my own perception of what I was doing evolved. A shift had occurred in Antigua when I adopted a greater sense of self belief, and it was in Bermuda I began to fully appreciate that what I was doing was something more than a big deal only to me. In the grand scheme of things my circuit on *Aluffe* did not amount to a peak of maritime achievement. There are plenty of examples of many more courageous and adventurous voyages. Relatively, however, my lone voyage across the ocean was still rare and out of the ordinary. As such, it tested the imagination and preconceptions of many of those I met along the way, and who offered their opinions accordingly. It was not by design that I found myself in that position, and I felt a little humbled by the attention which suggested a degree of self appraisal amongst the observers. For me to be dismissive of peoples reactions, be they knowing or otherwise, was to be disrespectful, and that, in Bermuda of all places, would just not do.

Tucked tightly against the shore at the head of the lagoon, the small dinghy club marina was the venue for a bustle of activity as visiting crews prepared their boats. Each of us watched the weather charts carefully, trying to predict the best time to set off on our respective journeys. I was heading to the Azores archipelago, 1800 miles over the horizon to the east, whilst others had their charts ready for a landing on the North American mainland to the west. Pursed lips greeted the birth of Tropical Storm Barry 1000 miles to the south-west, and its development was closely followed as it threatened to take a north-easterly course. We remained safe but the frontal systems spinning off the storm were quite vicious and rushed over the island delaying many departures. We were all looking for a weather window that would allow us to leave with some confidence of escaping being roughed up in the immediate days after slipping our moorings.

Many skippers had a frightening array of tools with which to predict the weather, often becoming overloaded with conflicting information and, consequently, almost incapable of making a decision. My policy was never to set off into a headwind, and not to concern myself with anything forecast much beyond 3 days. I used 2 specific websites only for information, along with the local synopsis chart, and some discussion with my dad. If the first 3 days looked positive and nothing horrible was predicted in the immediate days following them, I was happy and would be prepared to leave. Beyond those first 3 days I had always been resigned to the notion that whatever came along would have to be confronted. It was never likely that *Aluffe* would be able to outrun any threatening weather and so I had little alternative to adopting a frame of mind which allowed me to look forward to finding out what the bad stuff would be like. There was some trepidation, but the inevitability of bad weather made me take the more pragmatic approach.

Pragmatism was very much the glue sticking together the incredible achievements of a young Polish crew heading back to Europe having successfully found their way through the infamous North West Passage. Their tough 40 foot steel yacht was laden down with fuel tanks, tenders and other expedition gear strapped to the topsides. Struggling for cash at every step of the way, they were only the eighteenth yacht in history to have made it through the ice fields bordering the northern extremities of Canada. I joined a group in the clubhouse one evening for an impromptu presentation given by the young skipper, Tomas. He spoke of huge ice cliffs, polar bears, and revolting berry and whale blubber pie made by the native Innuits. A nearly disastrous 180 degree inversion during a storm off Alaska only heightened the crew's delight and self effacing excitement at what they had pulled off. Their story was inspirational for its grit and splendour. The thought of joining an expedition like that in the future was to occupy my thoughts often as I headed home.

Eventually, with the repairs completed, food stowed, and the weather favourable, I was ready leave on June 5th, 12 days after arriving. The only concern I had as *Aluffe* slipped away from the pontoon into the misty morning was for Mike who had yet to make a showing. It was clear from speaking to some mutual friends that he had left Sint Maarten 19 days before, giving him ample time to travel the 900 miles to Bermuda. During those days he would have undoubtedly run into some rough weather, but his boat was strong and he could have been expected to come through it trouble free. However, he hadn't arrived and, with reports of yachts being damaged and lost on that same stretch of water in the past weeks, I was not alone at the marina in being curious as to his whereabouts. There was no evidence to suggest the worst might have happened, and the Bermudan Coastguard had no information either way. It was not that Mike and I new each other well enough to be great mates, but he was another yachtsman and I knew what his plans were. As such I felt a duty to ask questions without causing any unnecessary alarm. It was possible that he had turned back or diverted to the Azores, but I was not to know and the answer remained hidden.

The legendary Bermuda Triangle, or The Devil's Triangle, refers to an area of sea commonly placed between the higher latitudes of the Caribbean, Bermuda, and the North American east coast. It has been the graveyard down the ages of many ships and aeroplanes, a number under allegedly suspicious circumstances. Magnetic anomalies and the supernatural have done their time in the docks of old as unexplained disappearances have mystified the analysts. It would seem, however, that its mythical status is not entirely warranted under the gaze of more modern analysis. In fact, the high number of casualties reported over the years is not disproportionate to other sea areas, given the volume of traffic passing through it. That the experts cannot agree on the perimeters of The Triangle – some stretch one corner as far as the Azores – is also a reason to avoid taking the more fantastical stories too seriously.

The reality is that the area is subject to the influences of Caribbean tropical storms, the Gulf Stream rushing up the eastern seaboard, and dangerous weather systems reaching out from the USA and the more northern Canada. There is no question that The Bermuda Triangle can be a devil of a place to be when things really kick off, but it is more deserving of a fearsome reputation than freaky. It was, therefore, something of a surprise to find Bermuda itself missing when I took a final look back at the island. With the arrival of a thick bank of sea fog the British overseas territory of Bermuda was no more only a short mile after *Aluffe* parted from its welcoming shores. If I had any concern for the welfare for its inhabitants, however, I didn't show it as I launched the large and colourful gennaker and high tailed it towards the east over a calm sea.

There is always a period of acclimatisation at the beginning of any voyage as one gets used to the motion and sounds of the boat. The new patterns to the day have to be followed and the restrictions of the cabin and deck have to be accepted. With each beginning, however, so the familiarisation process was being shortened. By the time the first evening meal came around I was already settled into the customary pace of life at sea on *Aluffe* and looking forward to the days and weeks ahead. I saw the leg as the one that was always going to provide the biggest psychological challenge, if not one in terms of sailing experience. From historical records and the published records of other sailors I could assume that the passage would not be as straight forward as travelling east-west on the more southerly route that I had come out on. The westerly prevailing winds were less predictable, and we could quite possibly encounter both harsh storms and flat calms before reaching land. How we would cope in either of those scenarios I had little experience to draw on but, as a gentle wind from the south-west eased us into our stride, any doubts were far outweighed by a maturing self-reliance.

Disaster struck early to test the high spirits on board when the external speakers I had bought for the ipod in Sint Maarten blew up. With the sun shining and *Aluffe* slipping along smoothly I was getting into something of a wild groove, singing and dancing in the cockpit. The Dandy Warhols' *Bohemian Like You* is a classy anthem but the speakers found the pace and, most notably, the volume hard going. It was a shock not to have got as far as establishing how much *I* liked *You*, before they gave an unannounced pop and then fizzled out for good. They steadfastly held out against my best attentions and intentions, remaining forever a reminder of the virtues of taking things steady. It was not a bad lesson under the circumstances but to do so is not to suggest that all excitement is banished.

Running the engine overnight I was alarmed at the sight of flashes of light coming from behind the engine cover. I leapt from my berth fearing the demise of my metal friend and the electrics, and pulled aside the cover. There was nothing to see at first and no acrid smell breached the barricades of my faulty nose. I watched carefully as irregular pulses of sharp green light leapt through the engine. I had no sense of danger or concern but was fascinated by the realisation that the engine was drawing phosphorescence from the sea and through the transparent pipes of the cooling system. It made for a simple but memorable light display.

The weather was subdued in the first 4 days, interspersed with short periods of no wind and the occasional thunder, but we still achieved an average 110 miles a day. I busied myself about the boat whipping the ends of sheets and adjusting the sails to suit the conditions. My understanding of what made *Aluffe* tick had improved dramatically since leaving the UK, as had the speed at which I could make changes to the sail plan. The foresail was now a simple operation using the lines led back to the cockpit. If we needed to sail goose-winged downwind, with the spinnaker pole holding the foresail to windward, I was able to set the pole uphaul and downhaul from the cockpit in advance of going forward. Checking the sheets were cleated so as to give me enough rope to play with, I would roll the sail in before stepping quickly up to the foredeck to attach the pole. Returning to the cockpit I pulled the sail out, now supported by the pole and providing more windage and balance on the windward side.

I was lucky with the mainsail in that it was small enough for me to take reefs in and out without having to alter course no matter how much pressure there was from the wind. As such, I would de-power it by releasing the kicker and some of the mainsheet before bracing myself at the mast. A quick adjustment to the reefing lines along the boom, and a tensioning of the topping lift to keep the boom end from dropping onto the deck, left me with only the need to release or pull on the main halyard. The whole operation could be done in a couple of minutes and never posed any problems in any conditions. Single line reefing led back to the cockpit, along with that of the main halyard, would have been quicker still, but I had always preferred the simpler option which would allow me to reach everything if the mainsail jammed up the mast. The simplicity of *Aluffe*'s setup paid dividends as the wind and sea was quite changeable in the northern half of the Atlantic.

A common route for sailboats from Bermuda to the Azores is to first head to the north-east in an effort to pick up the favourable currents and stronger winds. For a yacht to take the direct route is to take the chance of stalling in the windless Horse Latitudes, so called because of the unfortunate occurrences in the past when sailors were forced to throw their cargoes of horses overboard as food and drink dwindled. It was not that I had a horse on board I cared too much for to contemplate condemning it to the deep, but I really didn't want to extend my time at sea for any longer than necessary. There was as much desire to avoid getting stuck in a flat calm as there was being steam-rollered by a storm. *Aluffe* was carrying excessive amounts of fuel as a precaution but it was depressing to think of actually resorting to its use. Consequently, following the advice given to me by my dad, staying low to avoid dirty weather further to the north was making me more nervous as the days past. After 4 days, inching up when possible, *Aluffe* was tracking only a few miles south of the rhumb line and perilously on course for the historical dead zone when I called for the latest weather information, giving my position so a fix could be placed on Dad's chart.

"What are you doing there? You're much further east than I thought you would be."

"Well what do you want me to do, turn back?" I replied, slightly affronted that he was not bowled over with admiration at the blistering pace I had managed to extract from my steed.

"Yes, that would be a good idea. You're heading directly into the path of some seriously dirty weather with winds of 40 to 45 knots." He gave me the coordinates of a waypoint to head for, some 80 miles to the west-north-west.

I looked to the sky and saw little that suggested the immediate arrival of anything too hairy. "Are you sure or could I just continue on this course?" I was not so much challenging the weather charts or Dad's interpretation of them, but displaying a serious distaste for turning back on myself.

"No, no, I couldn't recommend that. It looks very nasty and you're heading directly towards it," he continued, pressing for swift action.

"How long have I got?"

"Is there anything to stop you altering course now?" I guessed he meant not long, and any further thoughts of being halted in equine soup were put aside.

The wind was no more than 15 knots in strength when I turned *Aluffe*. The sun was still warming the air through a soft mosaic of clouds. I drove *Aluffe* hard on her new course, but it was fairly obvious from early on in our flight that we would never cover the distance to the 'safe' waypoint in time. High above, cirrus clouds gradually overtook us, streaking ahead of a dark mass gathering ominously behind. The wind picked up steadily and I cursed my luck as *Aluffe* passed close by a small pod of pilot whales, riding with ease the mounting grey sea. Any other time and I would have slowed to enjoy the magnetic presence of these wonderful creatures, but matters at hand stole the moment.

As the afternoon ticked by and the conditions worsened there seemed no point in continuing. Far from being an act of surrender I could see that we were in for a pasting no matter where we put ourselves, so the best course of action was to give up the idea of trying to outrun the impending severe gale and get settled in advance of the worst. Reducing sail to 3 reefs in the mainsail and setting only a small section of the foresail, we hove-to. *Aluffe* had proven herself to be comfortable with this tactic before in gales, providing some justification that she would again, but I still could not be sure that this would work as well one notch up on the Beaufort scale. However, without any other more sensible options available I settled on the idea quickly without feeling the need to fret about whether I was doing the right thing. As evening closed in I used the fading light to get a hot meal inside me, check the location of my grab bag in the event of an emergency, and snatch some sleep.

By midnight the main front was on us and I was awake. *Aluffe* was held over at 30 degrees by the wind blasting through the rigging. It was not an uncomfortable position as the seas outside had been forced into a uniform pattern which *Aluffe* rode assuredly despite the buffeting from some of the sharper crests. The noise of the wind and water rushing over the deck prevented me listening to the ipod on the headphones. My thoughts worked themselves around the boat assessing its strengths and weaknesses in an effort to maintain a state of calm alertness. Cosseted in such a simple and small boat it didn't take long and I felt quite safe. There was really very little I could do but wait for things to settle down. As such I was relieved of the need to worry about not doing something and it was, therefore, relatively easy to enjoy the experience as one that doesn't come around very often. It was definitely my good fortune to be in that position and I pictured *Aluffe* from above, with me cocooned inside, riding the waves, darkness all around. Drawing my vision back until she was only a speck in the grand expanse of hostile sea, I swelled with pleasure at being in the middle of such outrageous and thrilling power.

6 hours past before there was any discernible weakening of the wind, and a further 4 before I wondered if I might be able to contemplate sailing again. Almost as the thought past through my head, without any warning, *Aluffe* was hit by the most fantastic force and shockingly loud bang. With the dying of the wind, the regimented lines of waves were losing their order becoming more confused. Unshackled, anomalies formed and *Aluffe* was hit by one of these bigger and breaking bullies. In an instant she was lying on her side at 90 degrees. There was no time to prepare myself and I managed only to cover my head as everything on the starboard side, including food and bottled water stowed in lockers underneath the berths, rearranged themselves on the port side. *Aluffe* did not stay down for long and resumed her position as soon as the wave passed. Thankfully I had been lying on my bed and not moving about the cabin or, worse, squatting over the bucket going about my morning ablutions. The shock of the knock down, however, still left me breathless and in need of throwing up. Clearly, despite my apparent calmness my nerves beneath the surface had become frayed with the persistent noise and shaking. Fortunately the protective cockpit dodgers had been partially ripped off during the storm and it was easy to lean overboard and rid myself of the tension.

Taking stock of the mess below - storage boxes upturned, lockers emptied, a galley knife embedded in the chart table inches from where my head had been – I was able to quickly re-stow most things. The loss of an avocado, which refused to reveal itself, was my only worry. Without a sense of smell there was a strong likelihood I would not notice as it rotted, and only discover a vile mess all too late. 3 days of regular forays into the forepeak failed to unearth it but I eventually found it in the early stages of decay, skulking under an old t-shirt in the closed side pocket of a kit bag.

If I thought *Aluffe* and I had received all the excitement we deserved, I was wrong. Resuming sailing in the early afternoon I drove so as not to risk embarrassing the Navic in the bouncy conditions. The wind was still blowing consistently at 25 knots from the south, and I had to steer carefully through the large waves coming at us from the starboard stern quarter. With only a small amount of sail up *Aluffe* still put on a good pace. With each slightly larger wave we were able to surf for a while, making for an exciting ride. After a while of helming in those conditions it is possible to sense the waves coming at the boat. Perhaps it is a case of understanding the sequence, a change of light and sound, or just peripheral vision that provides a warning, but when a big one comes along it tends not to be such a surprise. In a sea of 3 to 4 metre waves, one of 5 metres stands out.

Aluffe dropped further down the back of one wave into a particularly deep trough. It heralded the arrival of a big wave behind as *Aluffe*'s stern lifted first before drawing the rest of herself up and forward. There was a short pause and I held my breath. I think in that moment, as *Aluffe* hovered above the long steep face of the wave stretching out below, I got a glimpse of what a bullet in the breach of a gun, or an arrow nestling against the cheek of an archer, might feel.

"Here we go," I muttered.

Aluffe waited for the wave to take hold, and then she was away, skimming down and before the surge of water behind her. The tiller in my hands went light and the rig relaxed. The sails were still powered up but the pressure in them was greatly reduced as we shot forward, water pouring out to the side, *Aluffe* cutting through the water as if by right. Another large wave, from a less broad angle, rushed past, lifting *Aluffe* and depositing her back onto the top of the first wave. Off we went again on another blistering surf, during which I let out a loud 'Yaaa-hooo!' When my mood eventually matched the calming conditions I checked the top speed on my instruments – 20.8 knots. For a boat with a theoretical hull speed of only 6.5 knots, 20.8 is 'yahoo' indeed.

There followed nearly a week of frustratingly slow progress as

I struggled to get *Aluffe* further north with only the use of fickle winds and a seemingly adverse current. The storm had left behind a legacy in the form of an unpleasantly busy sea. The wind had dropped right off, fluctuating between 5 and 15 knots, but the sea state was like a mogul field set to shuffle. These were far from ideal conditions for *Aluffe* as she did not have the physical presence to stamp her authority. A wave would tip her bodily one way while another would catch her bow, twisting her before another pushed her forward or rudely smacked her stern. It was difficult to find a comfortable position anywhere on the boat and I often longed for something bigger that would provide an easier ride and carry more home comforts. With no way of improving the ride my patience was in danger of collapsing at times but to let it do so seemed slightly ludicrous with no-one around to register it. In those days I had worked out, and needed to remind myself, that part of long distance sailing involves lengthy periods of tedium and boredom. Bernard Moitissier would have no doubt relished the insight into the teasing nature of Mother Earth in her paddling pool, and Robin Knox-Johnston would have confronted it all with a plum duff and a slug of brandy. I, however, despite the valued insight into myself and offshore sailing, allowed myself to wallow in the more tedious moments and felt that I may have had more in common with Chay Blyth who 'endured' his rowing and sailing voyages.

As well as to relieve the boredom my intention had always been to use the time alone to read good books, including some of the classics that were long overdue a browse. On the long passage to Barbados I discovered Charles Dickens in '*Great Expectations*', and was absorbed by Andrea Levy's '*Small Island*' on route to Bermuda. Making for the Azores, as a distraction to the discomfort of the bumpy ride, it was quite apt that I should reach for '*War and Peace*'. Billed as the greatest love story ever written I had always suspected the publishers of being guilty of some hype or inaccuracy. I thought the longest or heaviest love story ever written might have been more truthful. As it was, I think we were both correct. The opening 400 pages saw us into more consistent winds and the final 1000 were completed at a gallop. Leo Tolstoy drew me in and I spent hours rising and falling with the emotions of his characters. Just as I was getting carried away with the written word so too was *Aluffe* thriving in the strong winds that had risen to meet us as we raced towards the cluster of Portuguese islands.

25 knot winds swung to forward of our beam. The Navic was faultless but the waves had a dark menacing presence about them. The heartening rich Caribbean blue had long since left the seas as we headed further east. I watched them carefully and the horizon in an attempt to predict how they might develop but they remained sinister in the main. When I was able to get reception on the satellite phone Dad was able to update me with the latest forecasts, all of which indicated a continuation of the same. *Aluffe* powered forward hungrily, eating up the miles as I devoured the Russian epic. The combined intensity of the sailing and the book was almost overpowering and sleep was easy to come by when I allowed myself to close my eyes.

I was deliberately pushing *Aluffe* in these conditions because they gave a perfect opportunity for her to prove her calibre. Holding a near perfect line through the waves she was like a horse given its head. Occasionally she took a hit from a larger wave but she was quick to shake it off, catch her stride, and dance forward. The pace was tiring but exhilarating as in 4 days we covered 500 miles, putting us within one calm day's motoring distance of tiny Flores, the western most island of the archipelago.

It is typical of the Azores to be blanketed by the 'Azorean High', an area of high pressure that creates often flat calm conditions. It is common practice for yachts, like *Aluffe*, to carry plenty of fuel if they are not in favour of a final creep to their destination. With the wind dying off and the waves finally subsiding, we motored the final hours, drying clothes and charging the batteries, finally dropping anchor in the small harbour of Porto das Lajes on the evening of June 23rd.

Many boats crossing to the Azores from the west go directly to the popular landfall of Faial, over 100 miles further east, and its comprehensive marina in the town of Horta. Choosing to stop first at Flores had been for me a decision based mainly on a wish to step on land as soon as possible. Walking in the hills of the volcanic island, however, why I was there did not matter. After months away from Europe it was surreal to be reminded so strongly of home by the lush scenery, singing birds and chittering insects even though the tranquil island was over 1000 miles from the mainland. Looking to the west the sky blended with the horizon in an imperceptible weld, sealing the excitement of the eventful past weeks forever in my memory. I lay in the long green grass of a hillside meadow with the sun on my face, the warm moisture of the ground making my clothes damp, and drifted away with the waves of hard earned tiredness washing over me.

Chapter 11
Three up to Spain

The picturesque harbour at Porto das Lajes is protected on one side by a large concrete breakwater, which in turn is guarded on the weather side by giant sized concrete tacks intermeshed to break up the powerful waves invading the island. On its other side tall black cliffs soar into the sky, home for thousands of shearwaters cackling and screeching incomprehensibly throughout the night. In between rests the anchorage with its clear cool water providing sanctuary for travellers at the end of their voyages. Nosing my way nearer to the shore on my arrival I noticed 4 smaller yachts grouped together in amongst the 15 at anchor and directed *Aluffe* towards them. Recognising a yellow, junk rigged Venturer 25 from the lagoon in Bermuda, I passed close by, and called over to the woman sitting in the cockpit.

"I saw you in Bermuda. How was your crossing?"

"It was alright but quite difficult at times. I got in yesterday." Shirley, from South Africa, was in her fifties and had set out a week in advance of my own departure suggesting that she had made slow progress through some nasty conditions. She must have seen me raise a quizzical look at the large grey cat half way up her wooden mast, because she added, "he slept below when it got rough."

"Very sensible," I replied, and arranged to meet her for a drink later at a bar in the village.

"Would you like some fruit? An orange? Or an apple?" These questions were being fired at me by an older man from a light blue Kingfisher 26 anchored close to Shirley. An example of each fruit arced over the water towards me and I managed to catch them before being drawn into conversation with Asmat, who had sailed alone from Surinam in 35 days. He was either tired of his own company or just had a lot of things to say, but, reminiscent of my arrival in Barbados, it was some time before I actually got around to dropping *Aluffe*'s anchor.

Wobbling my way unsteadily to the bar later I met with Shirley and Asmat. We were joined by an American, Chris, who sailed *Tradition,* an Albin Vega 27, and a young and enthusiastic French couple, making their way back to France after an Atlantic tour on their 26 footer. I had not been in the company of other small boat sailors for a long while and was impressed listening to their stories. Swapping experiences, the conversation was invigoratingly normal as each of us automatically appreciated where the other was coming from as a single-hander and/or small boat sailor. Shirley had spent 5 years on her boat travelling the world, and Chris was heading back to Ireland, from where he had set out for Brazil a few months before. The suggestion that any of us was mad had no place at the table, although Asmat had me pretty wound up by the end of the evening with his tendency for one-upmanship.

Speaking with Laurent, the young French skipper, it transpired that we had the same satellite phones.

"Ah, it is so useful to call home every so often and get the weather," he enthused.

"That's exactly what I use it for although, unless the sky is cloudless, reception can be pretty poor." Many of my conversations to home had been frustratingly put off or cut off mid-flow by the phone's refusal to pick up a signal unless the conditions were perfect. Even on days with no clouds in sight and with an unimpeded view of any passing satellites the reception appeared to be adversely effected by wind, which didn't seem to be right.

"Yes, you are correct, reception can be very bad and it was a month before I realised how to extend the aerial." Laurent sat back in his chair, drawing on his cigarette and nodding knowingly.

"You what? Extend the aerial?" I replied. All my efforts dismantling the telephone and disconnecting the aerial to clean the connections had failed in their own right to improve reception, but also to demonstrate that the latter could be extended at all. For 6 months Jacqui and I had suffered from a lack of communication and all because I hadn't read the manual. My only excuse was that the second hand phone came without a manual, but it was still quite lame.

Asmat, however, didn't care either way as he was adamant that satellite phones were as much an imposition on his freedom as were life rafts and flares infringements on his right to die. Pushing 60, Asmat was well travelled and very knowledgeable about many things. I know this because if he had one failing it was his inability to hide the fact, although much of it could be put down to his concerted effort to lure Shirley into his berth. His view that he had the right to sail his boat wherever he wished without safety gear and regulations forced upon him was a fair one for which I had some empathy. That idea of being a free spirit roaming the earth reliant only on wit and energy to survive in the manner of explorers of old is romantic and appealing. It ignores, however, the fact that in the 'good old days' wit and energy were not far off all that was available to the intrepid traveller. Given the choice, many of those would have packed away some of the vast array of safety kit on the market today if it reduced the level of unnecessary risk on their journeys of exploration. The extensive range of safety equipment available to sailors in modern times cannot be seen as bad for it saves lives. The continued growth of that sector is guaranteed for that reason alone. Detractors, however, will argue that the move to ensuring safety is part of an unwelcome trend removing a much sort after element of risk and, subsequently, some of the achievement, from adventure.

Moreover, the continued upgrading of 'must-have' kit does not always improve a sailor's chances of survival if a false sense of security leads him or her into waters well beyond their depth. There is a real concern expressed by many yachtsmen that the efforts to improve safety at sea is going too far beyond that which is necessary and reasonable, lowering standards of seamanship and removing, most importantly for Asmat, that essence of freedom sort by so many heading out to sea. Asmat's refusal, however, to carry even a simple VHF radio smacked more of obstinacy than principle. There was no need for him to put himself at so much risk of dying in the event of an incident to make his point. He applauded his own idea that for him to drown was his choice and within his right, which is technically correct but in so doing he would have proved nothing of virtue about either the free spirit, seamanship, or the will to survive.

Our seafaring forefathers went to sea for all manner of reasons including to fish, to trade, and to discover what was over the horizon. It is the same today but the times are different and it is futile for present day sailors to attempt to capture the real essence of sailing of old because we know so much more and have so many more resources available to us. We cannot ignore that entirely and expect to be credited. The sea can be a hostile and unforgiving environment which does not cater for those on a trip down memory lane or those trying to reconstruct the past. To sail offshore today without taking advantage of even the most basic safety equipment available within one's means is surely a wasteful and sad act of ignorance.

In a typically affable yachtie style an impromptu barbeque was organised on the beach the following evening to which all the crews of various nationalities in the harbour were invited. In between games of frisbee on the dark volcanic beach the collection of French, New Zealand, Canadian, American, South African, Surinam and English sailors once again proved that wine and freshly cooked food is a signal to welcome each other and share stories. Their tales helped to put into perspective my own journey. The ever present camaraderie amongst yachties is invaluable as a social and advice network. Its presence is indicative of the respect held by these maritime nomads for the enormity and power of the oceans. Every sailor runs many risks but the encouragement of one is the greatest support to the efforts of another. Amongst the laughter and revelry it was a sobering thought that my time amongst the transient community was only a few days sailing away.

"That must be a joy to tuck into after your trip," stated a Canadian who had recently arrived from the Bahamas with another Englishman. He was watching me make short work of a plate of potato salad and chicken, perhaps wondering if I had space for a cooker on board.

"It's very good but I eat pretty well when I'm sailing," I replied and explained how I had managed to lose a boatful of tinned squid along the way, replacing it with assorted instant rice meals and large American tinned stews.

"How about you guys, is it table cloths and fine cutlery all the way for you?"

"Not really. Peas are my favourite but my mate prefers spam."

"On their own?" I asked.

"Well, I like to mix some mustard in with my peas but that's about all we ate on the crossing. We don't like to use the cooker in case we spill hot food everywhere." It was an admission I had not expected and it made the paucity of my kitchen positively grand in comparison to their extreme approach to avoiding the washing up.

Needing to press on through the archipelago, which stretches nearly 300 miles from east to west, I left Flores the next evening in the company of the American, Chris. We both wanted to get ourselves organised in the main marina at Horta on the island of Faial but for different reasons. I was looking to give *Aluffe* another thorough check over in preparation for the hop to Spain, but Chris was meeting his girlfriend who was flying out from Ireland. It made a change to sail with another boat, not so much in convoy but at least in the same patch of sea, making for the same destination. I felt a buzz of excitement leaving the sociable anchorage behind to share the crossing with Chris. Although we lost sight of each other in the dark soon after leaving we both talked later of the perfect conditions that enabled us to cover the 130 miles in a little over 24 hours. I made it into the port a short while before Chris, tying up on the visitors dock in the early hours of the morning but, struggling to keep my eyes open, decided to get my head down. I assumed Chris would make it known when he arrived and I could help him tie up alongside, but heard nothing of his difficulties manoeuvring onto the dock a couple of hours later as sleep held me firmly in the bunk.

The next morning I announced my arrival in the Azores to the officials manning one of the 2 main customs and immigration offices in the islands, taking the opportunity to enquire about Mike. After his no-show in Bermuda I was of the growing opinion that he had diverted to the Azores in the face of bad weather. If he had done so the office in Horta would have it noted.

"No, Senhor, there is no mention of your friend Mike or his boat in our records."

I had hoped for something different from the search of the recent records of boats arriving. Short of contacting the Falmouth Coastguard station, with whom Mike would have registered his boat in the event of an emergency, my options were limited. There were still many possibilities as to his whereabouts but not so many ways of finding out, which was a nagging worry. Making my way into an internet café to send emails home I also sent one to some friends who knew Mike from Dominica, asking if they knew of someone with whom he might have been in contact. Returning to *Aluffe*, I concentrated on fixing the tiller stock – an important block of aluminium connecting the tiller to the rudder - which I noticed had started to come loose in the final days before reaching Flores.

The marina in Horta is extremely well organised, catering efficiently for the needs of the many yachtsmen who pass through during each season. Situated behind 2 breakwaters it is a popular safe haven in the worst of storms, although only a matter of weeks before I arrived the pontoons had started to break up with the passing of some atrocious conditions. Quick thinking crew's lashed boats together and saved the marina from becoming a scene of carnage but, at the corner of each finger pontoon, fresh oversized welds were evidence of the marina office's determination to prevent a similar situation developing again in the future. Its most impressive feature, however, was the view it offered of Pico, the dormant volcano rising resolutely 2350 metres out of the neighbouring island, also called Pico. The almost perfect cone was often topped in ventricular cloud giving it not only the appearance of a nun's habit, but also an irresistible appeal. Chris, his girlfriend Karen, and I decided to climb the mountain before we sailed home. 2 young Kiwi brothers, Jon and Paul, swelled our expeditionary group to 5. Part of the attraction of sailing is that it is a great way to reach places worth exploring and each of us saw in the mountain a challenging opportunity not to be ducked. The idea that we should watch the sun set and rise from the top was Jon's, but he didn't need a hard sales pitch to convince us of its merit.

Leaving *Aluffe* behind we crossed the short distance to an anchorage on the north coast of Pico in convoy. Joining the brothers on their 37 foot boat I got a shock stepping on board at the sight of the cockpit covered in blood.

"Ah, we caught a big tuna on the way here and it got a bit messy cutting it up. It'll clear up alright, don't you worry," Jon explained matter-of-factly, adding genially, "Welcome aboard."

That 'function before form' was a guiding principle for the brothers was self evident, and I was quick to learn that it was a defining quality of their characters and the trip they had undertaken.

Buying their boat, *Double Bruyn*, in Florida for a pittance they had patched it up in time to sample the delights of the Bahamas before setting off on their stated aim to reach Europe. As befitting 2 lads in their twenties, their early wanderings were laced with the obligatory tales of love, beer and song in the sun, but along the way they were forced to overcome a series of near catastrophic gear failures. In the Bahamas they drifted for 3 days while they stripped out the entire steering gear to secure the rudder which threatened to detach itself. Within a week of the start of their Atlantic crossing the autopilot packed up leaving them with no choice but to steer alternately for 3 hour shifts for the remaining 2 weeks. Not long afterwards the starboard shroud, one of the 8 wires holding the mast up, ripped part of the main bulkhead off which had been secretly rotting away with time, courtesy of an undiscovered leak through a window. Some hasty patchwork saw that complication off and technically they had reached Europe by landing in the Azores but still had nearly a thousand miles to go before they could step on the mainland. Looking up at the rigging and the assortment of additional ropes being led back from the spreaders to secure points at the stern, I wondered if their troubles were over. Apparently not, as Jon explained.

"Ah, yes, well after the autopilot broke I noticed that the backstay was fraying, so we had to drop the mainsail and tie these ropes to the mast to stop it falling over. It wasn't too bad actually. The boat sailed really well on just the genoa."

"Are you going to fix it here and then go on?" I asked.

"We'll see. We're a bit skint right now and need some money. We haven't really worked it out yet, but we're thinking of leaving the boat in the Azores and coming back after we've worked in Europe. I'm sure we can find a boat heading to England, or somewhere, from the marina."

As down to earth and interesting guys I thought it very likely that they would be snapped up as crew without any trouble, keeping their plans alive.

With the afternoon long in the tooth our window of opportunity to reach the summit in time was fading with the light, but we were soon heading to shore with a random collection of clothes, food and wine to sustain us overnight. Even the best laid plans founder on rocks and so we should have not been so surprised when the outboard jumped off the back of the brother's dinghy and sank in 40 feet of water. A frantic paddle against a strong wind pushing us out to sea ensued and I climbed aboard *Tradition*, leaving Jon and Paul to figure out a way of retrieving their truant engine.

In the initial excitement of the moment Jon was all for diving to find it amongst the rocks and weed, which was all very well, but lifting it was another matter. As 30-somethings, Chris, Karen, and I tried to pass off our greater years as wisdom, pondering the options calmly while Jon enthusiastically donned long fins and a mask. He disappeared for minutes at a time without locating the engine, adding weight to the growing suspicion amongst us sages that its loss would have to be put down to an expensive learning experience, before he surfaced once more, this time carrying the engine. The bizarre incident left us laughing but, with a drowned engine to strip down and clean immediately, it killed any hope of climbing the mountain that evening.

Pico does not require great skill to climb but, as mountains tend to be, it was steep and so I was both surprised and pleased that the 1500 metres from the start of the walk to the summit the next day was not too arduous. Reaching the lip of the wide moonscape crater it was a short scramble up the final nipple, from where we could appreciate the benefits of height. Not having done much walking in the past months and having spent all of it very much at sea level the view from the peak was all the more rewarding. Standing with a clear blue sky above us and looking down through holes in the fluffy blanket of cloud below, *Tradition* and *Double Bruyn* appeared as mere specks in the anchorage. The islands were obscured behind the cloud and haze but not missed in the glow of achievement and grandness always offered by mountains.

"Oh, Happy Days!" Karen stated on everyone's behalf.

Returning to *Aluffe* by ferry the following morning I relaxed in my seat, chuckling at the final moments when I said goodbye to the Kiwi boys. Jon was preparing to run me ashore in the dinghy while Paul was aloft checking the rigging for any weaknesses.

"Ah, Jon." There was a rare trace of deflation in Paul's voice.

"What's up, bro?"

"Mate, this rigging's bad. We're going to have to change it all."

Jon smiled at me. "Ah, well, we'll sort something out."

I had no doubt that they would. Theirs was a particularly crisis laden path but, given the value of *Double Bruyn*, the state of their finances, and the extent of their ambition, it was no surprise to them. As a consequence they were prepared to solve each setback and did so without fuss or complaint. They had been good company and I hoped to catch up with them later on the island of Terciera, which would be my departure point for Spain within the week.

Continuing the tradition of crews visiting Horta I painted *Aluffe*'s logo on the marina wall and left for Terciera 70 miles away before it was dry. Chatting to Chris and Karen while I indelibly marked *Aluffe*'s presence there was an element of sadness in the thought that I was parting from valued friends again. Fond memories of our trip to and up Pico would often be recalled and I was pleased that a solitary climb up the mountain had not been forced upon me. The thought of being able to telephone in the future and say 'Do you remember .....?' was a cheery one but also signified that those memorable times were over and never to be shared in my own home.

The ancient town of Angra do Heroismo on Terciera is famous for its baroque splendour captured in the plethora of ornate castles, churches and palaces. Artistically formed balconies and tiled buildings are features of the town which is a designated World Heritage Site for the long history and culture it represents. Mooring up after a night sail my subdued mood matched that of the town's but only because its inhabitants were knackered after a week of celebrating The St John's Festivals. Hiring a scooter I toured the island along well made roads lined with thick blue hydrangea bushes. An attempt to meet up with the Kiwi's in Praia da Vitoria on the opposite side of the island via a forest road ended in near disaster with its sudden end and the start of a large water pipe. Returning to the main road I eventually caught up with Jon and Paul, as they prepared to head into a local village to run with bulls.

Unlike bull fighting, its running counterpart as practiced by the Azoreans only on Terciera does not require the services of a flashy matador in a packed stadium, and thankfully dispenses with much of the gore, although there are definite similarities. A simple village with most of its residents hiding behind a heavily fortified street is sufficient as a venue, with the street being the track down which the bulls run. Instead of the professional showman it adds spice to an evening if a bunch of ignorant yachtsmen are mixed in with some of the more brave or drunk locals and told to run towards the bull with the intention of getting it really angry. The first bull needed no such encouragement and scattered all before him over walls and into ditches, as did the other 4 bulls that each had a 30 minute run. One larger animal, despite the best efforts of 8 men – the mascarados da corda - on the end of a rope trying to drag it back, achieved a minor victory by forcing its way into a crowded bar, emptying the panicked contents through windows into the street in seconds. It was a high octane evening with the scars and grazes to prove it but why Paul and I ended up dancing in a fountain I cannot recall.

Sitting at a pavement bar in the early hours drinking coffee, water dripping off our wet clothes and forming puddles around us, Paul lifted his head in my direction and looked at me through tired eyes.

"Hey, Will. Wouldn't it be just great if Jon and I came to Spain with you on your boat? Man, that would be awesome!"

I had been mulling the idea over in my head for a couple of days myself but Paul prevented any further discussion on the subject by falling asleep in his chair.

Moving with *Aluffe* to the marina in Praia da Vitoria introduced us to an Irish family and one from Northern Ireland. Between them they had 3 children with the oldest being 14. I had met a number of families on my travels which convinced me of the value to children of going to sea. The opportunities to learn about different cultures and their languages, the natural environment, physics, engineering, the universe and everything seemed boundless and entirely positive. The need to make friends quickly with virtually anyone that comes along is a great skill for all people to have but one of necessity for the traveller amongst strangers. All the children I met were friendly, confident, enthusiastic and street wise beyond their years. It was not a case of them losing the innocence of their childhood early, but being on boats and having new experiences in foreign lands appeared to make them more open to change and accommodating of differences. It seemed fairly obvious to me that boats were a good thing for children, even if the truth remained hidden to some of them at the time.

"You must feel really lucky to be sailing with your family." I was talking to the 11 year old Donnacha from Ireland while he explained what he would be doing as the self-appointed Master of Ceremonies at the origami party I was to host that night on *Aluffe*.

"I hate it," he quickly spat the words out. "I hate it."

"But surely it's fun to meet different people, see different places, and learn languages? What about all the sun?" I said, hinting at the good times.

"It's rubbish. I don't know why my parents took me away. They should have left me at home. I don't have any friends because we always move about, the weather has been awful, and as for the language, it would be a lot better if everyone spoke mine. Now, watch this carefully, this is a swan." He took a blue sheet of paper from the little used origami set given to me by my brother to stave off boredom on the longer crossings, and made a number of intricate folds.

His swan was excellent but I remained slightly disappointed by his attitude to the virtues of a life on the sea.

"I expect not many of your friends at home have been travelling like you. Don't you think some of the difficulties are worth it for the opportunity you've been given?"

"Let me tell you, the only good thing about all this is the money."

"You've been paid to go sailing?" I was shocked.

"Not exactly, but before we left everyone but my parents could see it would be rubbish for me and gave me money to make up for it. I made 300 euros in the end off my gran, and aunt, and other people. That was really good." I rallied a little at this, albeit slightly mercenary, positive result.

"Excellent, and think of the stories you can tell when you get back...." I started, hoping to impress on him the value of taking in as much as he could in the meantime, but was cut off in mid-flow.

"That can't happen soon enough. I'm telling you, if we don't leave in the next 3 days I'm taking the next flight home. Now, I'm off for my tea but I'll be back in a couple to set everything up. Look after my whale for me while I'm gone."

"Right-ho." I said.

Our conversation was not the ringing endorsement I might have wished for my theory about mixing children and boats, but behind Donnacha's statements lay proof of an advanced self-awareness and capability. Perhaps he had them anyway but his experiences on the sea were in no way to their detriment.

The idea of holding an origami party had arisen after Donnacha let it be known how good he was, and could even create shapes without the need for instructions. 14 people crammed themselves into and around *Aluffe*'s cockpit. Handing out slips of paper MC Donnacha instructed and berated us in turn, cajoling from his audience various origami shapes, figures and forms. Somehow he engineered it so that we all won prizes for our labours although his father, Declan, for offering what appeared remarkably like a square piece of paper, can consider himself fortunate.

Under the weight of all those people the boat sank low at the stern, forcing water back through the drain hole in the cockpit until there was nearly 6 inches of water covering everyone's feet. A guitar, fiddle and an accordion appeared as accompaniment to the steady consumption of cheap wine and beer until 3 o'clock in the morning. With only a few hours remaining before we left it seemed for *Aluffe* an appropriately bizarre send off. It wasn't necessary but no less heartening to have confirmed by a happy and partially inebriated Irishman that my choice of crew for the leg to La Coruna in north-west Spain was 'cracking'.

"Those Kiwi boys are special and you're set with them on board," he smiled.

There was a temptation for some to think that the decision to offer the boys a lift was a spontaneous one fuelled by alcohol and poorly thought out. The fear was that *Aluffe* would be overcrowded and together we were being carried away by the apparent craziness of the idea. On the contrary, I was initially against it on principle for to carry extra crew was to break the solo element of my plans. The fact was, however, that I felt enough had been done to prove to myself that I could cope with solo sailing, despite some of my hang ups about solitude. My skill and competence around the boat had improved dramatically, making me comfortable with the notion of long passages.

But the trip was taking us back towards the busy shipping lanes and it would be useful to have extra eyes and hands on board approaching the mainland. To have them with me would make for an interesting late twist in the adventure, and the chance to share the experience with others could not be underestimated. Besides, they were becoming good friends and it didn't seem entirely necessary for a little thing like *Aluffe* to put a stop to that. For 3 days I kept my thoughts to myself and, apart from Paul's solitary enthusiastic outburst, was put under no pressure by the boys to take them. *Aluffe* – short, thin, low in the water and carrying only a simple rig – was not to many people the ocean-going yacht of choice. For Jon and Paul, however, she encapsulated an essence of adventure to which they could relate. Function before form mattered most to them and, after an invitation to lunch during which we rehearsed cooking a meal together in the confines of the cabin, they willingly threw their lot and a small kit bag in with me.

A final check of my emails revealed that Mike had eventually arrived in Bermuda, one day after my departure and 20 days after leaving Sint Maarten. A collision with a whale had left him with one badly damaged hull on his catamaran which he was able to partially mend before nursing his boat slowly to the island for more substantial repairs. My belief that Mike had always been safe was supported by an equal measure of hope. Logging out of my email account with the news that he was indeed alive and well was a satisfying way to sign off from the Azores.

Setting out on July 9th for La Coruna, 900 miles over the eastern horizon, any potential loss of speed from carrying extra weight was offset by our ability to fly the large spinnaker or gennaker without fear of being short of hands to manage them. We settled into a rotating pattern of 3 hour shifts at the helm having decided not to bother with the Navic. The advantages of having with me experienced sailors was immediately obvious. It was not a case of letting my guard down but, whereas before it was never possible to switch off, I was now able to partially hand responsibility for the boat over to whoever was on watch. Sleep was easier to come by and my appetite, far from suffering, expanded with a corresponding interest in cooking large quantities of simple hot food without any of the fiddly bits. Fortunately, the boys brought with them a large pan and the same attitude towards meals as I, although Jon rather spoilt the united front by his ability to drag out the pleasures of a mini sized Snickers bar for a whole night. Paul and I barely got the wrappers off before swallowing them whole.

In typical fashion we made excellent progress in the first 5 days covering nearly 600 miles. Each leg of my trip built on the experiences and lessons of those preceding it, and I began to feel more in harmony with *Aluffe* and the condition of the sea than ever before. On the second morning I was standing at the helm with the tiller controlled between my legs, sailing on an easy sea into the rising sun while Jon and Paul slept below. In my left hand I held the sheet of the spinnaker and in my right the guy. Aluffe slipped smoothly through the water, balanced and assured. It was an involuntary laugh of happiness that escaped from my throat in response to the warming sun on my face and the feeling of contentment conjured up by the magical moment.

"What's up?" Jon asked from his berth.

I smiled broadly back. "This is a special time. I'm loving this. Happy Days!"

"Yeah, it's good, Will." The fact that I got a reply was the best bit.

The potential issue of conflict through lack of space never arose as we settled quickly on an understanding of what was required to make the trip a success. Our expectations of comfort and personal space were suitably low, as befitting our meagre accommodation. We were also fortunate in that Jon and Paul were naturally suited to sailing on *Aluffe*. In describing Paul one could think of the All Black rugby team and imagine him to be a flanker, tall and solidly built. Most importantly in light of his stature he displayed an extraordinary talent for falling asleep wherever and whenever it was required, therefore negating any discomfort afforded by the cramped conditions. For his part, Jon might be considered more of the team mascot and as such was able to squeeze into any remaining nook or cranny. When the 3 of us sat together in the cabin space was at a premium and conditions were cramped. However, this rarely happened as the weather was kind to us in the main and one person was nearly always on the helm, while one or both of the others rested below. When we were all forced to take refuge inside it was plainly understood that we had to be more careful and considerate. The only slight issue that did arise was Paul's regrettably literal interpretation of the boat's 'Bucket and Chuck It' sanitation policy. After squatting on the appropriately named Poop deck at the stern of the boat he failed to keep hold of the bucket when dispatching his offerings to the deep. No amount of indignant shouting and abuse encouraged him to swim after it or for it to miraculously jump back on board. We could have turned the boat around and practiced our man-over-board procedure but whatever Paul had put in the bucket did nothing to improve its ability to float and it was soon heading far below. Fortunately another bucket was produced and we were able to continue on our way without any lingering embarrassment.

As a newly fledged skipper my early attempt to establish what our roles might be and how the boat should be run was successful, if short lived, when Jon looked at me and revealed, "Whatever, Will, we'll do anything. We Kiwi's aren't here just to fuck spiders."

Being such nice boys, I really hadn't thought they were but it was fortunate that they weren't and had other qualities because on the sixth day the very important tiller stock, the same one I had repaired in Horta, disintegrated. The wind had been picking up with the arrival of some wet weather. That the tiller was becoming sloppier each day had not gone unnoticed but Jon made particular mention of it to me when he handed over the watch at midnight. The boat was balanced and tracking well in the waves but I was slightly alarmed that there was nearly 2 inches of play in the tiller at its tip either side of the centre line. Driving *Aluffe* in the depreciating conditions was a good test of my ability to pre-empt the effect of waves and gusts but not something that needed to be explored for long.

"Guys," I called through the closed hatch, "we're going to have to heave-to and sit this out until the morning. We'll have to check out the problem tomorrow but I can see that the block is cracked and loose."

"Good plan, Will. Let's get some sleep."

From many of the photographs we were able to take during the following 30 hours spent hove-to fashioning a repair it might seem that I played a leading role in getting us underway again. I can be seen filing, sawing and administering liquid metal to critical parts, generally being a hero skipper getting his young crew safely back home under testing conditions. In truth I did little more than make some porridge and a cup of tea at first light before following instructions handed out by Paul. It was the sensible thing to do given that he had spent 5 years building super-yachts in Auckland before meeting up with his brother in America. As for Jon, seeing a need to secure the free moving rudder in the 2 metre waves, he jumped overboard with a rope between his teeth leaving me with the important task of handing him a towel when he climbed back on board.

Viewed in a certain way it is possible to think that the Kiwi boys were too ready to take unnecessary risks in pursuit of adventure to the point of being irresponsible and a danger to themselves. Their yacht, *Double Bruyn*, was beset with problems indicative of a boat that had received little in the way of tender loving care prior to being sold on the cheap. The argument that she was not seaworthy enough to cross an ocean holds some water even though she proved herself to a point by getting as far as the Azores. However, the mindset of Jon and Paul, coupled with their practical skills, sets them apart from many 'normal' sailors and should excuse them from the scorn of aficionados who might accuse them of being negligent in their preparations and carefree about the associated risks. They did do a considerable amount of work on *Double Bruyn* before they left Florida and carried many tools but, as every boat owner will testify, it is never enough and something can always go wrong at sea, and invariably does. Their greatest asset used to offset the problems they faced was their attitude in a crisis, which personified calm and resourcefulness. They were under no illusions about the dangers of crossing an ocean but had the skills and composure that permitted them to believe they would succeed in reaching Europe.

It was a justifiable belief for we successfully completed the repair and drew into La Coruna on the evening of July 18th. There we found the showers to be hot and the beer cold as we celebrated our passage and the completion of Jon and Paul's first ocean crossing. I would never have thought it possible but the ever present smiles on the boys faces actually got bigger and their teeth, brushed regularly after each meal and before bed with almost religious zeal, shone even more brightly. Happy days.

Chapter 12
Trials, tribulations and home

Stopping in Spain was supposed to be a brief affair but bad weather contrived to keep *Aluffe* tied up in the marina for 6 days during which time my mood got progressively more gloomy. The waiting I could handle as I had at the very least learned to be patient with the weather. However, with Jon and Paul departing for Holland and Mallorca respectively in search of work, I was more aware than ever that my own trip was soon to end. One more leg, 4 days, and 500 miles would see *Aluffe* back in Cornwall after nearly a year away in foreign climes. There were times along the way when I felt stressed by events, missed Jacqui, and wished to be amongst old friends. On those occasions being so close would have been a comfort but they had been rare moments on a trip that had given me new insights into the natural world, human behaviour and my own emotions on a daily basis.

At school I spent many a long lesson staring out of the window, distracted by a wish to be elsewhere. At the time I always saw this lack of concentration towards the wise words of the teachers as my failing. They in turn, and perhaps not unfairly, always had me pegged as a pupil that 'could do better if he tried'. I have since come to believe that such opinions highlighted an unfortunate misunderstanding at the time and I was, in fact, in the wrong classroom. English, history and geography are all fascinating subjects which my teachers taught well but my interest and imagination lay largely outside the restrictions of formal education. From the first moment the idea of sailing around the North Atlantic came into my mind I had been absorbed to the point of being single-minded. The subject matter enthralled me straight away and the desire to learn more was only matched by my willingness to put in the effort in order to do so. If *Aluffe* was my desk, the North Atlantic was the classroom in which was provided for me the best education. In such a rich learning environment and in contrast to my younger days, by the time Spain was reached I had no wish to be anywhere else.

Being 2 hours ahead of Greenwich Mean Time Spain confused me with its schedule and the fact that the good townsfolk of La Coruna insisted on loading their days at the back end. Habitually I would get up in the morning soon after first light. It was a hangover from the Caribbean when the heat of the day soon discouraged any serious activity, but also the first opportunity in every 24 hours on passage to check the sea was still reassuringly wet and blue. La Coruna tested that regime by setting the clocks so that it was almost 7 o'clock before the dawn was permitted to appear, and steadfastly refused to open the doors of the cafes for a coffee until gone 9. Shops, offices, and pedestrians took much of the morning before there developed any sense of purpose, whereupon they all closed for a long lunch or buggered off for a kip, depending on whether they were a shop, office or pedestrian.

By the time a buzz returned to the city centre I was due for my evening feed but, with many of the restaurants withholding service until the setting of the sun, the clocks were hinting at a new day before my hunger was satisfied. Walking back through the town in the earlier hours of the morning to *Aluffe* and bed after a long day waiting for something to happen hundreds of people would invariably be spilling out of bars and filling the streets dressed to party the rest of the night away.

I tried on a few occasions to join in but quickly became distracted by my continual thoughts of returning home and soon lost interest. The last leg was relatively short but potentially packed with excitement and some danger in the form of ships, poor weather systems and, of course, The Bay of Biscay. It was not so much, however, the need to psyche myself up for that challenge that restricted my good humour but more a case of just being upset that a fantastically rewarding journey was drawing to a conclusion.

Carrying out the checks on *Aluffe*'s rigging and fittings had become routine and I moved quickly about the boat satisfying myself that all was as it should be. More than ever I felt at ease and at home in the small cabin, which seemed suddenly all the more spacious and accommodating without the boys and their kit. All that I needed to ensure my comfort and the efficient progress of *Aluffe* I could find quickly without any struggle to remember where it was located. *Aluffe*'s appearance in the marina, tucked in amongst the larger yachts resting part way through their journeys, was no longer that of the precocious upstart of old. This time she carried about her an air of belonging that comes from the experience of spending thousands of miles at sea. Likewise, it was not with the normal excitement that I studied the weather charts, searching for the right moment to cast off for the final time, but calculated the task more dispassionately.

As the days and hours ticked by the chances of making it to Fowey, my intended destination on the Cornish coast, by July 28th narrowed. Jacqui and my family were hoping to watch me arrive at some point during that day but with every low pressure system sweeping in from the west bringing with it strong winds and large swells the problems of nailing a convenient arrival time became pronounced. Much as it would have been nice to see them on the pontoon as I pulled in, my priority was not to take any unnecessary risks at that late stage. It would have been too easy to have got carried away with the excitement of the occasion and make a mistake before the line was crossed.

Eventually, at midnight, after a day of grim squalls and rain, I checked the charts and decided to leave at dawn a few hours later in the knowledge that 3 days of forecast steady winds would get us level with Ushant off the north-west tip of Brittany. After a short rest, and as the last of the party-goers was tripping their way to bed, I guided *Aluffe* clear of the confines of the quiet harbour and headed north. The approaching dawn lifted the early morning gloom and doused the lights of La Coruna that dropped away behind. The next stop would be home and my thoughts on that were as turbulent as the enormous swell, residual evidence of the rough weather over the previous days, which accompanied me throughout the morning.

With little wind at first to help us we motor sailed through the uncomfortable conditions until a steadier breeze picked up and the sea settled a little. Another yacht, a solid motor-sailor by design, ploughed past rolling ponderously through the swell. From the position of a lady draped over the stern with her head in her hands I didn't get the impression that we were any worse off for being small.

During the day there was no let up in the number of ships constantly in sight. Our departure from La Coruna had been in the company of a fleet of inshore fishing vessels and a swarm of seagulls, but as the day wore on I was wary of the larger trawlers and coasters that appeared indiscriminately over each horizon. Sailing into the night and closer to the shipping lanes running north-south the ships disappeared from view but isolated lights moving silently through the dark revealed their presence.

Sleep had always been a fitful affair on passage but on this occasion I permitted myself only blocks of 30 minutes before waking and checking carefully for ships. If a light was spotted in the distance its position was closely monitored to ensure our paths would not cross before I snatched another 30 minutes. It was a hard regime and one that I was forced to maintain day and night throughout the passage as the visibility deteriorated with the arrival of a disturbingly thick fog. Noise does not travel far at sea and large cargo ships are eerily quiet anyway, and can appear undetected worryingly easily. It is one of the reasons why solo sailing has always courted controversy and I did my best not to fan the flames by keeping a keen watch on the blanket surrounding *Aluffe*. In those conditions there are many psychological games at play to reassure oneself that nothing will emerge dangerously from the gloom but I opted more for the 'what you can't see, won't hurt you' approach. In terms of quashing all my apprehension it was not a fail safe measure for it still allowed for the possibility of a collision, even if in the event I would be unaware of the unfortunate disaster.

"All ships, all ships, all ships, this is yacht *Aluffe*, yacht *Aluffe*, yacht *Aluffe*." I called the message out twice over the VHF radio before continuing.

"All ships, this is yacht *Aluffe*. I am sailing in poor visibility without radar." I completed the message giving my position, course and speed, requesting that any ships in the vicinity make themselves known. Silence. Despite sending the message out every hour no reply was ever returned and I eventually gave up trying, reverting back to a constant vigil and playing the odds.

When tiredness became overwhelming and I estimated *Aluffe* was safe in relation to the track of vessels in the shipping lanes I dropped below for a reviving nap. The danger of assuming anything at sea were highlighted after one of those occasions when I calculated that no ships could realistically be expected to be travelling on a route that threatened our position. Settling back on my berth I glanced one final time through the window and suffered a sharp moment of alarm at the sight of a rust streaked hulk ghosting past only a short distance off to port. It had been nowhere to be seen minutes beforehand. Taking a positive slant on the situation I chose to ignore that particular lesson and assumed that every ship would keep a healthy distance between each other, which gave me a chance to grab a few minutes of untroubled sleep.

The fog thankfully lifted on the third day but was replaced by high winds from the south-west approaching gale strength. The waves grew larger by the hour and I reduced sail gradually to allow the Navic a fighting chance of maintaining control. The biggest worry was our position some 20 miles due south of a point at which the steep continental shelf is reached. From there the water depth would drop from 4000 metres to 100 metres in only 30 miles. Along the length of the shelf the waves would bunch up and could make life very difficult and even dangerous while the wind was still goading the waves to greater proportions.

There was still a hope of reaching Fowey in daylight the next day and it was tempting to press on regardless of the rough seas that would be encountered over the shelf, but such risks were unnecessary at this stage of my trip when I was so tired. With the gale set to continue for the remainder of the day *Aluffe* had to be slowed for fear of reaching the shelf before the gale blew itself out. It proved to be an opportune moment to test another storm tactic, that of running before the wind trailing behind a bunch of fenders on the end of a long warp.

Carefully sorting out the lines I attached 3 fenders and let the line out. *Aluffe* responded well to the delaying tactics and the Navic was grateful for the extra drag enabling it to hold a steadier course against the disruptive influences of the waves. I had reduced the sail area to a minimum but still *Aluffe* was averaging over 3 knots - slow for us but too fast under the circumstances and so 3 more fenders were threaded down the warp. Biting into the waves some 40 metres from the stern the 6 fenders slowed *Aluffe* to a little under 2 knots and made her progress steadier again. Deliberately going slowly was counter intuitive and it confirmed that I could not possibly make it to Fowey as planned. Nonetheless, it was a responsible decision easily taken for all the right reasons and I was pleased that the challenge to press on had been resisted.

The 'go slow' tactic worked perfectly as the wind died off before the depth dropped significantly. The waves also subsided so that our cross over into the relative shallows of The Western Approaches and The Channel was uneventful. Rounding Ushant outside and to the west of the formal shipping lanes at midnight on 27th July I had nearly 24 hours to go before *Aluffe* would make her final stop on our tour. The whole of that night and the following day was spent keeping a watchful eye on the numerous ships passing close by on their way to ports near and far.

"Where are you?" Dad asked when I called at midday for a weather forecast.

I told him.

"Right, well you can expect a Force 7 and a lot of rain later on. I'm sorry we won't see you today but be careful and we'll be on the quay tomorrow morning first thing."

He was right. The weather did turn progressively wet and nasty during the afternoon. *Aluffe*'s speed increased with the ever increasing wind pressure that mirrored the wind of the day before. Rain pelted down as I put 3 reefs in the mainsail and set only a scrap of headsail. Visibility was again cut to a minimum. I had the assurance of the Falmouth Coastguard that no ships over 100 tonnes were close and none was heading towards me, and so I continued. Had we been in the open sea, as we were 24 hours before, I might have hove-to or slung my fenders over board to calm the situation, but not this time. It was a 50-50 decision whether to slow down or head for a safe port.

On the one hand The Channel was an inhospitable place to be in a gale at night where sharper waves and other vessels of all sizes were potentially serious threats. On the other hand, being driven closer to shore by a ferocious onshore wind was hardly the safe option. In the end it was the scent of home that won the day. We were south of The Lizard, the southern most point of England, in the early evening with nearly 40 miles to run to Fowey. The Cornish coast was hidden from view by heavy rain and low dark clouds ripping eastwards to the tune of the harsh wind.

It occurred to me that our final approach to every one of the destinations on our circuit had not been straightforward. Mostly we had been forced to motor the last hours under flat calm conditions. Nazare, La Gomera, Barbados, the Azores and Spain were all examples of that frustration. Bermuda had given the impression that she did not want us to arrive for a while but eventually relented in the early hours of the final morning. This time, for our final destination and home, we were going to have to work all the way to the line.

Aluffe leaped forward with each powerful gust, surfing at every opportunity as the conditions continued to deteriorate with the descent of darkness. Without extra crew and stores of food and water, *Aluffe* was lighter and therefore more agile and responsive than she had been at any stage. The Navic could not cope in the strong following sea leaving me to drive *Aluffe* as I would a dinghy, seeking out the best line through the waves. Almost 2 years before *Aluffe*, Jacqui and I had been caught in strong winds heading to Salcombe. That occasion had been the catalyst for my trip and I approved of the coincidence. With Fowey somewhere unsighted ahead it seemed appropriate that the whole experience should go the full circle and be signed off in a similar fashion to how it had all begun.

The second time, of course, was different. Since that hairy September day in 2005 I had come to know every part of *Aluffe* intimately, the sea was no longer the unfamiliar territory it once was, and my level of seamanship reflected the accumulation of nearly 10,000 sea miles. For all the thrill of our first encounter, it was a highly charged and emotional ending. The thrashing *Aluffe* and I were subjected to was like an exam, a test of all that we had been taught in the past months. Like any student who has paid attention and prepared well I welcomed the trial and found myself shouting for more as another squall ripped through the rigging.

I was, in many ways, ready to stop. *Aluffe* had become too small for me and I was tired of living in a state of semi-curl on board her for so long. Her lack of stability and general motion was wearing after so many months and the appeal of space and greater home comforts was tangible. The desire to catch up with friends and family was strong. Knowing that they were so close made me welcome the sight of the coast when it eventually showed itself as the weather relented. With the lights of Fowey beckoning only a few miles ahead, I couldn't help patting myself on the back, proud of what *Aluffe* and I had achieved for ourselves.

But the final hours being blasted home from The Lizard was also a time of great angst. My exhortations to the wind to blow harder and stretch me further were those of someone who had become content with the sea environment, at ease with its rhythms and beat. They were a gauntlet thrown down by a confident student to his teacher demanding the opportunity to prove himself. They were the distressed cries of someone who knows he is soon to suffer a great loss. They were my prayers that the journey would not end.

Finally, however, the end did arrive as *Aluffe* passed St Catherine's Castle protecting the entrance to Fowey Harbour. As we did so the moon shone brightly through a gap in the cloud, lighting up the rocky shoreline. It was momentarily tempting to think it was a sign of recognition from someone or something watching over our efforts but that would have been fanciful. Instead our arrival went unnoticed by the sleeping town of Fowey and its neighbouring village, Polruan. I was grateful for that as it allowed me the time to gather my thoughts and rest a little before catching up with Jacqui and my family a few hours later over a champagne breakfast.

The highly charged emotions of the preceding hours were replaced by a quiet satisfaction at having completed the circuit. Despite the best intentions of the wind mine was not a glorious dash for the line in the style of an explosive sprinter but the almost inevitable result that could be expected by any deserving endurance athlete that has prepared well, taken one steady step at a time, and paid attention along the way.

Picking a careful line through the day boats and other assorted yachts tugging on their moorings, I tied up on a spare buoy. Light bursts of rain continued to fall intermittently from the clouds scudding by overhead as I hurried to pack away the sails and lines. Sleep, although much needed, would not come so easily without going through the ritual of tidying

Aluffe's decks and rearranging the cabin, the customary signs that our passage was completed.

Before dropping below I glanced around and spotted the low, thin lines of an Achilles 24. Looking at her small mast rising neatly up from her cabin roof I wondered how far her potential had been explored. Had she ever been to France or the Isles of Scilly? Further? The little boat swung lightly on her mooring, responding quickly to the vagaries of the wind scuttling around the enclosed harbour. I suspected not but could understand why. She really did look very small.

'But big enough,' I added.

Having successfully returned to Cornwall and achieved what I had set out to do, many were generous with their greetings and praise, often adding that they felt it appropriate then to let me know that they had always thought I was quite mad. Such sentiments matched the persistent 'Are you mad?' theme that accompanied me around the Atlantic and dogged my preparations.

Aside from moments in that first week out of the Canaries, from the outset when the thought initially occurred to me I never doubted that such a trip was within our grasp. At the time my lack of offshore sailing experience was matched only by an inexperience of boat maintenance, but I was neither a novice nor an idiot. *Aluffe* was undoubtedly small but, as a design, she had an offshore pedigree in which I could trust. It was a sound basis from which to work.

It is not technically difficult to sail across an ocean. The skills required to do so are known to the majority of club sailors and coastal cruisers enjoying their sport and recreation around the world. The chances of crossing without drama are greatly improved if some basic planning is undertaken. If I had run into really bad weather it would have been unlucky given that I chose to sail the particular legs during specific periods, those that avoided seasonal storms. It does take some nerve, however, and more so if the choice is to go it alone. How much nerve will depend on the individual and their personality. It will not necessarily be the adrenalin junkies who will take it in their stride. Alone and distant from any support means that a high level of calm resourcefulness is required but in many cases it will not be until one is in a desperate situation that one will know if those characteristics are owned. It is near impossible to simulate such experiences in training and so not a small amount of self-belief will always be an asset where the unknown and how to respond to it is the greatest challenge once, of course, the courage to actually go has been mustered. For would-be 'explorers' it is the pressures and expectations of modern western society that can shackle them to the shore and pose the most problematic of barriers that must be scaled in the first instance. Such a barrier can be maddening and should not be underestimated.

Having committed myself, the enormity of the task did not escape me. What was required to prepare *Aluffe* and I for the rigours of the ocean was plain enough. A growing conviction accompanied me as each hurdle was overcome. Even when I struggled with depression soon after leaving the Canaries the fact remained in my mind that many others had successfully challenged themselves in similar ways before and would do so in the future. I was not so different to them and there was, therefore, no real reason why I could not work through those difficult times and emerge all the stronger. Such moments had always been anticipated and, on reflection at least, welcomed for all that they taught me about patience and perseverance in an occasionally hostile environment. Many lessons are harshly learnt but that does not stop us from trying. If it did creativity would be stymied and ambition would be a thing of the past in a poorer world.

During the trip I enjoyed the company of whales, the very sight of which made me go weak at the knees. Dolphins were a common presence playing on *Aluffe's* bow wave and at night their songs drifted through the hull as I was rocked to sleep. At each busy marina and secluded anchorage strangers welcomed us with genuine friendship and kindness. I snorkelled in the clear, warm waters of the Caribbean, and my tan was deep and long-lasting. Vivid sunsets and sunrises sandwiched a billion stars at night. I had experiences, both good and bad, that stretched my limits, extended my horizons and made for the best education.

As anyone who attempts a similar journey will find, there is no such madness as the reaction of others to one's own sanity.

Acknowledgements

One does not spend 2 years planning, preparing for and executing a journey of this nature without the support of many, many people. It is simply not possible to pull together and survive the undertaking without the practical and moral assistance of family, friends and strangers. The merest level of interest shown by a soon-to-be ex-work colleague at a low point in my preparations was enough to boost my level of persistence at the critical early stages. Likewise, the tired welcome of another customs official satisfied enough my need for recognition after the completion of another leg of the journey. That little things make big differences was a feature of sailing on *Aluffe* and so it was true with the value I attributed to the abundance of genuine smiles of welcome and offers of support along my way. I am indebted to all those people who to this day have no idea how appreciative I am that our paths crossed.

Getting *Aluffe* into some semblance of order over the Winter of 2005 and then Spring and Summer of 2006 required an almost constant presence in the St Winnows boatyard where I benefited entirely from the cheery and unflappable support of everyone else there busy fitting out their own boats. Many a problem was solved by the impromptu loan of a power tool, pair of hands, or piece of advice. Frank, owner of the yard, never appeared to mind me making my own space in his tool shed. It would have been a disaster if he had and I am grateful that he didn't. Without the presence at the entrance to the yard of Angie's café serving the finest homegrown burgers and cream teas I would surely have wasted away with my exertions.

It was not often that I called for the assistance of friends but the offers from Jez to help were frequent and invariably timely. The mast, dodgers, self-steering, engine and log all have his mark on them and make me wonder why he didn't come along to help in the galley. He would have been welcome. Matt, Greg, Molly, Jon, Paul, Chris, Karen, Kieran, and the medley of Atkins, all managed to appear at just the right moment on the circuit to keep my plate spinning.

In writing this account I have been fortunate to have received the helpful guiding comments of David, Nick, Jez, Jeremy, Polly (1), Polly (2), Laura and Catrina.

To voluntarily leave behind loved ones to complete what is unquestionably a selfish trip is a big deal but far greater was the willingness of Jacqui to let me go with her support. She convinced me that I was on the right path, keeping me sane during the stressful times and allowing me the space to focus on the preparations when I needed it.

Finally, a deluge of thanks are due to my parents who have been unwavering in their commitment to me and the trip, a trip that provided them with more than a few sleepless nights but also one into which they threw their lot. It would have been a far greater undertaking without their considerable generosity.

WG

Lightning Source UK Ltd.
Milton Keynes UK
21 September 2010

160157UK00001B/39/P